D0509637

a hands-on guide

# HANDMADE

a hands-on guide

# HANDMADE

Make the things you use every day

## ASA CHRISTIANA

The Taunton Press

The Taunton Press
Inspiration for hands-on living®

The Taunton Press, Inc.
63 South Main Street, PO Box 5506, Newtown, CT 06470-5506
Email: tp@taunton.com

Editors: Carolyn Mandarano, Peter Chapman
Copy Editor: Candace B. Levy
Indexer: Heidi Blough
Art Director: Rosalind Loeb
Cover Design: Barbara Cottingham
Interior Design and Layout: Stacy Wakefield Forte
Photographer: Asa Christiana, except as follows: David Bertman (p. 187: top left), Erin Berzel (p. 104: center left and right, bottom), MJ Ferreri (p. 136: bottom), Timothy Hamilton (p. 149: top right), Kari Merkl (p. 187: top three photos on right), Mike Pekovich (pp. 132, 134), Coby Unger (pp. 41: bottom right, 43: all), Jacob Wener (p. 187: bottom right), Matthew Philip Williams (p. 187: bottom far left and bottom left)
Illustrator: Dan Thornton

The following names/manufacturers appearing in *Handmade: A Hands-On Guide* are trademarks: 3M®, Adobe®, Amazon®, Arduino®, Barcelona®, Best Buy®, Birchwood Casey®, Bluetooth®, Brasso®, Burning Man®, Cameo®, Craftsman®, Craigslist®, DeWalt®, Dick Blick Art Materials®, E6000®, eBay®, Etsy℠, Festool®, Floating Bed®, Forstner®, Fusion 360™, Goo Gone®, Goodwill®, Google™, Grizzly®, Handler®, Hobart®, Houzz®, IKEA®, Illustrator®, Instagram®, iPhone®, Kreg®, Lego®, Loctite®, Lucite®, Lynda.com®, Magic Eraser®, Maker Faire®, McMaster-Carr®, Mod Podge®, Mold Star™, NatureServe®, Netflix®, Onyx™, Oracal®, Photoshop®, Pinterest™, Quikrete®, Rust-Oleum®, Sakrete®, Sharpie®, Simple Green®, Smooth-Cast®, Sony®, Speedball®, Starr™, Sterno®, Super Glue™, Sure Cuts A Lot™, Tandy®, Tarvol®, Waldorf®, Walkman®, Wells Fargo®, X-Acto®, Xbox®, YouTube™

Library of Congress Cataloging-in-Publication Data

Names: Christiana, Asa, author.
Title: Handmade, a hands-on guide : make the things you use every day / Asa
   Christiana.
Description: Newtown, CT : The Taunton Press, Inc., [2018] | Includes index.
Identifiers: LCCN 2018023885 | ISBN 9781631869341
Subjects: LCSH: Handicraft.
Classification: LCC TT157 .C473 2018 | DDC 745.5--dc23
LC record available at https://lccn.loc.gov/2018023885

Printed in the United States of America
10 9 8 7 6 5 4 3 2 1

About Your Safety: Using hand or power tools improperly or ignoring safety practices is dangerous and can lead to permanent injury or even death. Don't try to perform operations you learn about here (or elsewhere) unless you're certain they are safe for you. If something about an operation doesn't feel right, don't do it. Look for another way. We want you to enjoy the handcrafting, so please keep safety foremost in your mind.

## dedication

To my wife, Lynne, and the world we've built together

# ACKNOWLEDGMENTS

This book would not have happened without the advocacy of Peter Chapman at The Taunton Press. The new handcrafted movement blurs boundaries and crosses lines, and I appreciate Peter's willingness to work outside the usual categories. I also deeply appreciate the careful work of this book's editor, the talented Carolyn Mandarano, and the creativity of its layout artist, Stacy Wakefield Forte.

My deepest debt is to the 15 makers featured herein, who reflect the diversity, generosity, and fearless inventiveness of this worldwide movement. They signed onto the book's mission without hesitating and went to great lengths to give me everything I needed. Their websites, blogs, and social media handles are listed throughout, and I encourage you to visit and connect.

I must also thank two well-connected people who helped me chase down many of the makers and artisans in this book. Matt Preston, communications director at ADX (adxportland.com), connected me to a half dozen talented teachers and practitioners. And my longtime friend RH Lee, who manages Nick Offerman's cooperative woodshop in Los Angeles (offerman woodshop.com), hooked me up with the folks at Instructables (instructables .com) in San Francisco and thus a whole galaxy of amazing makers.

I would also like to thank *Fine Woodworking* for letting me adapt Scott Grove's article on molding, which I edited and shot when I was on the magazine staff, as well as *Woodcraft* magazine for doing the same with an article on welding that I produced in 2017.

Then there is my talented friend Duane Bolland, who is always ready with his camera (or chainsaw) when I'm in need.

And last, creative careers are taxing on more than just the creators, and mine wouldn't be possible without the love and support of my wife and kids.

# introduction

**WHEN I TOOK OVER** as editor of *Fine Woodworking* magazine in 2008, all of us on the editorial staff were worried. The big real estate investment bubble had just burst, which devastated the economy, and magazine subscriptions were an easy place for people to cut costs. But the truth was, our sales numbers had been sliding for a few years already. Every survey told us that our graying readers were aging out of the craft—and their magazine subscriptions—more quickly than we were replacing them with 20- to 40-somethings.

There were powerful factors at work, like the rise of the Internet, the demise of shop classes, and the exporting of skilled factory work—each one more lasting and threatening than a temporary economic depression. The market would recover, but the world of handwork might not. We placed our hope in the cyclical nature of life, put our heads back down, and worked to keep the craft alive.

## THE FIRST CRAFT REVIVAL

The history of *Fine Woodworking* reads like the history of the craft movement. The magazine's launch, in the mid 1970s, coincided with a rediscovery and reinvention of woodworking and handcrafts of all kinds. With *Fine Woodworking* leading the way, a coalition of hands-on hippies, corporate dropouts, doctors, engineers, and others embraced the hobby as a way to do something personal and meaningful. Finding a market for their work, many turned pro.

The fledgling magazine, along with a pile of publications about getting back to nature and rediscovering traditional skills, were part of an acknowledgment that something had been lost in the hyperconventional 1950s and 1960s.

Taunton Press followed up *Fine Woodworking* with magazines for passionate gardeners, cooks, homebuilders, and sewers. Part of what made this craft movement happen is that many readers showed up with skills already in hand.

To those of you who grew up in the 1990s or later, it's hard to explain how different things were before then. Here's what matters most for our purposes.

The overall standard of living was lower; most kids had shop classes, which existed to prepare them for skilled factory jobs (mostly relocated overseas now); and instead of the Internet, cable TV, Netflix, YouTube, and video games, we had four crappy TV channels.

We played board games and tinkered with things to pass the time and save money. Folks fixed their own cars, houses, and appliances. And you didn't need a term like DIY when everyone was doing it: growing veggies, canning produce, hanging clothes on clotheslines, knitting, crocheting, sewing clothing, and scrapbooking (before it was a thing).

Growing up in the 1970s and 1980s, I caught the tail end of the old culture and the front end of the virtual age. Until I was about 10 or so, my scruffy little friends and I built forts from scavenged boards; hacked together our own bikes; and built model cars, boats, and rockets. The rockets were the coolest, with launch pads and black-powder engines that shot them into the clouds and little parachutes that brought them safely down again (into trees and on roofs mostly).

We were more bored than today's kids, but luckier in some ways, because we made our own fun.

## ENTER THE INTEGRATED CIRCUIT

After the microchip hit the mass market, nothing was ever the same. I was 9 or 10 when I saw my first video game. Pong was nothing more than two rectangles batting around a square, but for a generation of digital virgins, it had all the addictive power of today's immersive RPGs.

More games followed, with video arcades in every strip mall and home equipment most parents could afford, and we spent more and more time staring at screens. Things only got worse (and better) when cable TV and video-rental stores arrived. I remember staying up all night watching MTV in its first year, watching nothing more than music videos.

> **Arising out of "hacker" culture and a new rebellion against passive consumption, the first self-proclaimed "makers" emerged.**

The microcontroller had a massive impact on jobs too, making automation possible. Slowly but surely, jobs went from hands-on to hands-on-keyboard, and shop classes started disappearing. At the same time, fewer parents used tools and did things by hand so kids had less exposure to those things.

Mind you, I'm not judging later generations for being less handy. If I had an iPhone and an Xbox growing up, I don't think I would have built much of anything.

But here's the thing about building with your hands: Life's not the same without it.

If you view humans along an evolutionary timeline—picture a rope miles long—modern society is a little knot at the very end. For eons before this brief era, our survival depended on our ability to use tools and make things by hand. In fact, we evolved to do those things well, better than any species on earth. Like staring into a fire or sleeping outdoors, those activities are in our instinctual memory.

That makes the handcrafted life essential to who we are and an urge that can't be tamed, which takes us to the next chapter of our story.

## THE INTERNET FIGHTS BACK AGAINST ITSELF

As editors of a leading craft magazine, we saw the Internet as both friend and foe. On one hand, it was a powerful and exciting new tool for communicating and teaching, letting us add video, daily blogs, a podcast, and a much more interactive relationship with readers. But the Web was also our biggest competitor, enabling a growing, generous community to give away for free what we were asking people to pay for. Type any woodworking question into Google, and pages of links come up for videos, projects, blogs, product reviews—not always as clear and reliable as the carefully curated content from *Fine Woodworking*, but free, ranked by popularity, and multiplying daily.

We were also in a pitched battle for our readers' time. People were spending more hours than ever at work (we were told the chip would do the opposite!) and when they got home, they had a dozen ways to unwind without leaving the sofa.

I was so busy toiling away in my silo trying to stop the slide that I didn't notice the maker movement until it was a few years old. Outside our traditional niche, something amazing was happening.

Arising out of "hacker" culture and a new rebellion against passive consumption, the first self-proclaimed "makers" emerged, at first reprogramming and transforming digital devices but soon using new digital tools like 3-D printers and laser cutters to create entirely new objects and devices.

These new makers needed wood, metal, leather, and power tools to make their steampunk creations come to life, and a rediscovery of traditional crafts soon followed.

Today, *maker* is a big umbrella with fuzzy edges, including both digital and analog modes, pros and hobbyists, practical projects and crazy stuff made for fun—with traditional crafts and trades somewhere around the perimeter.

Making it all possible: the Internet, a mind-boggling matrix of connections and capabilities, where a worldwide community can explode exponentially, sharing in real time. Makers range from artisans who turn their nose up at the word to inventors and creators who embrace it, making things no one could have predicted. Tying them together is a sense of satisfaction that's a million years old.

As a writer, I love the irony of microcontrollers and the Web being used to fight back against the digital age.

Outside the maker world, the movement back toward a hands-on life is taking many forms. For some, it's a return to home-cooked food with fresh ingredients, guided by YouTube; for others it's as simple as puzzles, adult coloring books, or wine-and-paint classes—each delivering a bygone sense of steady, satisfying handwork.

If you doubt that the new movement is real, check out the explosion of handcrafts on Etsy and Pinterest, explore the scores of DIY channels on YouTube, and scroll through massive, crowd-sourced websites like instructables.com. The numbers are staggering, and for a longtime maker like me, sweet relief.

What is different this time around is how non-judgmental makers are. The new movement is a celebration, and all are welcome. So are mistakes, which are the best teaching tool of all. So there's no pressure to be perfect, and you are free to try anything.

## INTO THE NEW FRONTIER

In 2015, I left *Fine Woodworking* and headed west to Oregon, to hang up my shingle as a freelance journalist and maker (plus climber, hiker, biker, and all-purpose adventurer). It was scary but exciting, a chance for me to move outside the narrow world of fine furniture and start building without boundaries—like makers do, like I did when I was a kid.

In truth, I've never seen a division between remodeling my house or making the stuff that goes in it, between taking an afternoon to build a funky desk with plywood and plumbing hardware or laboring for two months to craft a chair with fine hardwoods and traditional joinery.

Step one in my transition was creating a woodworking book for a new generation who grew up without the chance to learn the basic skills that make so many projects possible. So I wrote *Build Stuff with Wood,* published in 2017 by my old friends at Taunton.

Assuming zero skills, limited space, and a limited budget, I used only a few small portable power tools to build all the stuff in that book. At the same time, I made sure every project was stylish, sturdy, and totally useful—in other words, doable yet well worth doing. The best part was ignoring the old conventions and working like makers do, using oddball supplies and putting things together in unconventional ways.

With *Handmade: A Hands-On Guide,* I'm all in. This book has been an amazing opportunity to learn about all sorts of new materials and modes—concrete, leather, digital tools, Arduino, welding, casting, printing. I hope it's the same for you.

I worked hard to vet the projects for that same mix of style and simplicity I went for in my first book. There are millions of DIY projects online, but not all are as doable as their creators claim, and others just don't work or look that great when you're done.

Out in Oregon we love our ales and lagers, and I see this book as a beer flight—a rack of little glasses that let you try all sorts of flavors in short order. I'm sure you'll find something you'll love.

—*Asa Christiana*

# 1

# join the maker revolution

**CAUGHT UP IN THE MOMENT.** Time slips away when I'm in my garage workshop making things.

**YOU MIGHT NOT THINK SO,**

considering how much time we spend staring at screens, but we are living in a Golden Age for handcrafts. In a deliciously ironic

turn, the same Web that has captured so much of our attention and free time is powering the trend back toward something real.

When the digital era first arrived a few decades ago—video games and cable TV at first, then the Internet, social media, YouTube, and all that followed—it dealt a crushing blow to the hands-on life. All you had to do was look around your neighborhood to see fewer people working on their homes and gardens, fixing things for themselves, and doing crafts like woodworking.

But the urge to make things by hand is an ancient one, and it refuses to die. As best we can tell, *Homo sapiens* walked upright onto the world stage about 200,000 years ago, with a genetic lineage that extended millions of years further back. That makes modern society a mere instant in human history. We evolved—body and mind—to resist the brutal forces of nature by hunting, gathering, making and using tools, and mastering all of the materials we could find. Our survival depended on it.

I argue that much of what makes us truly happy contains echoes of that evolutionary history: love, laughter, cooperation, outdoor living, feeling self-sufficient, and making things with our hands. For most of us, digital natives or not, these essential experiences are more deeply satisfying than pressing buttons and swiping screens.

Building things unites your body and mind in a single task, forcing you to focus on the moment, slowing your chattering monkey brain to a more methodical, peaceful pace. You were naturally selected to love building.

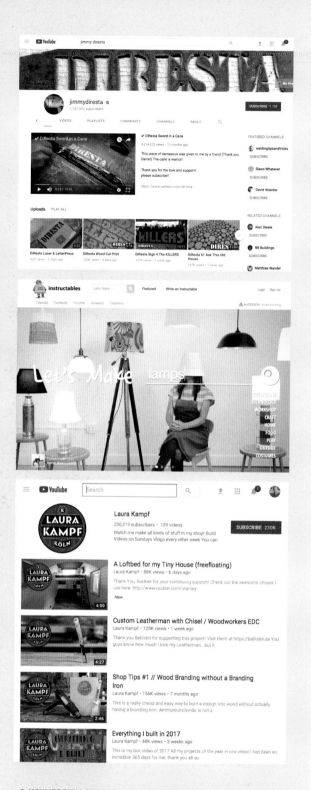

**A UNIVERSITY ONLINE.** YouTubers like Laura Kampf and Jimmy DiResta draw hundreds of thousands of subscribers with a winning blend of authenticity and creativity. And crowd-sourced sites like instructables.com will teach you how to build almost anything.

# POWER.OF.THE.NET

Like any tool, the Internet can be used for good, bad, and everything in between. The whole time it was rendering us helpless, it was also feeding a rebellion. Inspired by the hacker movement and empowered by the Web, a new generation of makers began using digital tools like 3-D printers, laser cutters, micro-controllers, and circuit boards to build things on their own, outside the reach of corporations. Soon they were mashing up their projects with wood, metal, and other materials and rediscovering traditional crafts.

While, admittedly, most modern citizens are still heading toward those floating recliners at the end of *WALL-E* (a must-see movie for readers of this book), there are unmistakable signs of life. Etsy has exploded with artisanal goods. Makerspaces and community workshops are popping up all over. School systems are learning that STEM (science, technology, engineering, math) doesn't stick as well for students without hands-on experience, and shop classes are making a comeback under hip new titles like *engineering*.

For more on this modern revolution in handcrafts, how it's different from the craft movement in the 1970s, and how it's the same, see the Introduction to this book. What matters most is the common thread that unites all handcrafters: the desire to build something rather than buy it.

The motivations behind that desire are many. One is a general rebellion against globalized mass production and the dominance of multinational corporations, chain stores, and consumerism. Maybe even more powerful is the urge to reclaim something that was lost.

Chris Gardner (p. 145) got hooked on handcrafts a decade ago and now runs two influential DIY blogs that extol the handmade lifestyle. In many ways he's a poster child for the modern movement and understands it from the inside. "Making the objects we use every day is a fundamental way to connect to the world," Chris says. "I grew up in a generation when shop class and home ec weren't even offered as courses; we were raised on fast food and given breakable plastic for birthdays. Our parents and grandparents tried to give us the convenience they never had, but we ended up surrounded with disposable objects."

"The real allure is self-reliance," says Timothy Hamilton (p. 157), who teaches printmaking at ADX, the big makerspace in Portland, Ore. "When you make something for yourself, you get more than just the object. There is an experience in making—in challenging yourself, learning new skills, and gifting what you've made—that can be more valuable than the finished project could ever sell for. Makers don't see the finished project as a final destination, but more like another step and jumping-off point to the next."

# NO BETTER TIME THAN NOW

Even if you are starting from zero, not sure what a drill bit is, or why a drill needs one, you have more advantages than obstacles at this moment in hands-on history. Whatever you're into, there is someone demonstrating it on YouTube: woodworking, Arduino, CAD, welding, leatherwork, or turning a cargo van into a gypsy lifestyle (#vanlife).

Looking for inspiration? Scroll through Pinterest. Cool projects and step-by-step advice? Try Instructables (instructables.com) and a hundred other blogs and sites, some hosted by the makers in this book. When your toilet won't flush or your faucet leaks, Google's got you covered. If you want to touch and feel before you buy and create, there's the ubiquitous home center, a cavernous cache of building and craft supplies ready be transformed.

## easy access to tools & supplies

The Internet puts an unprecedented array of supplies at your fingertips—cool stuff like rare-earth magnets and LED strips, hard-to-source hardware for

**SELL WHAT YOU MAKE.** The explosion of Etsy users is evidence of the recent revolution in handcrafts. You can set up a storefront in minutes and buy some of the supplies you need, too.

handcrafted lights, and vintage items for your steampunk creations. Just browsing will give you great ideas.

And tools are cheaper and easier to acquire, too, with the wisdom of the crowd and the power of the Web serving up best buys for every task.

## more ways to sell your work

If you aspire to sell what you make, the barriers have never been lower. You can set up a web portfolio and online storefront in an afternoon and harness the power of social media to connect with customers around the world. Embracing the new appetite for artisanal goods, new-breed craft fairs and funky storefronts are showcasing independent craft and design.

**THE HOUSE NUMBER THAT LAUNCHED A BOOK.** This sign lets you know you've found MakerFlat, a guest house in Portland that's furnished with handcrafted furniture and accessories of all kinds. As soon as I saw the stainless-steel screws acting as pixels, I knew that the maker movement needed a book of projects like this one. The sign (and MakerFlat) is the brainchild of Bryan and Jen Danger of zenbox design.

You can try Japanese woodblock printing once (p. 147), hang your handmade art on the wall, and then sell your carving chisels on eBay. Or you might dive deep into a craft and get really good—and maybe even start selling your work. In this new maker mindset, however, not every project needs to lead somewhere. It's enough just to say, "I did that."

With rigid trades and traditions outweighed by a spirit of adventure, there's no shame in being a beginner. No one knows everything, so there just aren't many know-it-alls, and mistakes are embraced as part of the journey.

That's not to say some makers aren't as skilled and experienced as any architect or traditional tradesperson. Ezra Cimino-Hurt of Case of Bass (p. 27) has a design sense honed in art school, a facility with materials from his days as a pro builder and remodeler, and an amazing ear for audio quality, all packed into every unique boom box he builds.

As one of today's makers, you can dabble freely or dive deep. Or both.

## RISE OF THE MAKERSPACE

Among the evidence of a growing movement is the rise of the makerspace. If you're part of the urban migration, you'll likely find one in your city. Numbering 1,400 worldwide, these new community workshops range in equipment and focus from STEM training for kids to hacker labs for adults.

## NEW RULES (NO RULES)

Everything from the most basic to the most expert advice is out there on the Web. That means you don't need trade school to try something. You don't even need to pay for a class, though in-person experiences can shorten your learning curve and be a lot of fun.

Unlike the old days, when motorheads stayed under the hood and cabinetmakers stayed in their shops, everybody does everything now. The makers in this book shift easily between casting concrete, cutting wood, and soldering circuits and are likely to mash up all three.

**BUILD WITHOUT BOUNDARIES.** The new revolution is more about creativity and fun than staying in your lane.

The typical makerspace offers a mix of digital fabrication tools and industrial-quality equipment for woodworking, welding, jewelry making, printmaking, sewing, and more, plus a robust educational program for all of the above. That's exactly what I found inside Portland's big maker hub, ADX, which also rents dedicated workshop space, hosts weekly events, and acts as a mecca for the craft-curious and craft-committed. Basic membership is affordable and gives one access to all the tools, plus a cut rate on classes.

For Chamisa Kellogg (see p. 181), a freelance illustrator who came to Portland in 2015 "looking for my people," ADX is much more than a well-equipped workspace. "It's 75% of my social life," she says. "There are lots of creative people in their 20s and 30s, and it's really fun to see what everyone is doing and to have a network of people I can turn to."

A related resource for urban makers is the tool library, where a fee system or membership gives you access to equipment you can take home.

Of course, community workshops have existed for decades, inside woodworking guilds, community colleges, retirement complexes, and more. As I traveled the country shooting projects for this book, I encountered all sorts of them, from a woodworker's club in San Francisco to a digital fab lab in LA set up in a complex of artists' apartments, each designed with an industrial workspace at floor level and a small apartment at the top of a spiral staircase. Dreamy.

# PLACES TO LEARN AND WORK

In my travels for this book, I visited lots of community workspaces. Some teach traditional crafts, some specialize in digital tools, and some do both. You won't need a community shop to do most of the projects in this book, but if there's one near you, you should check it out.

**WHERE MAKERS MEET.** Portland's vibrant makerspace, ADX, is just one of the active community workshops scattered across North America and Europe. It offers the latest digital design and fabrication tools plus a wide range of industrial tools for traditional crafts—and a robust education program for all of the above. Most important, ADX is a community hub where creative types can find each other, work side by side, and share what they know.

**SHOP SPACES ABOUND.** Richard White showed me around the San Francisco Community Woodshop, where members can take classes and use all the tools and machines. I know of dozens of other woodworking guilds, community colleges, and similar organizations with open-access workshops and classes. The same goes for ceramics and many other traditional crafts.

**DIGITAL FAB LAB.** The Build Shop in LA has 3-D printers, laser cutters, and other powerful digital tools you can use on your own or with expert assistance. It's part of an artisans' compound with upstairs apartments and downstairs workspaces.

**SIMPLE CAN BE GOOD.** Just by screwing some IKEA legs onto a slab of plywood, I made a cool deck table (right). The hanging planter for succulents wasn't much harder (above).

# WHY BOTHER?

Flip through this book and you'll learn how to make things you use every day, feeling more powerful and self-reliant as you go. It takes only a taste to get hooked. Like Spider-Man, when you get bitten by the bug, you are endowed with superpowers and changed forever.

You'll find yourself fixing things instead of throwing them away or hiring somebody to fix them for you. That will keep a surprising amount of cash in your pocket. We're on our third house, and each time I move into a new one and start remodeling it, I learn more about what's going on behind the walls.

Each new project rounds out my knowledge and skills: building a deck, installing trim, turning a basement into living space—and most recently, remodeling two bathrooms, complete with new shower stalls, tile, toilets . . . everything. I asked a contractor friend to help me with the first bathroom, and then I tackled the second one solo.

Last year I built my own backyard fence—a 120-ft.-long mix of wood and galvanized metal, which fits right into my Portland neighborhood. A little bit of determination and hard work has saved us tens of thousands of bucks and turned our apartments and houses into homes. The Danish concept of *hygge* is hot right now. Loosely translated, it means "cozy, charming, and warm." Handmade is 100% *hygge.*

You'll notice a fair bit of pride seeping through the previous paragraphs. There's no denying it: One of the best things about making stuff is the bragging rights. People tend to notice things that are handmade or custom and ask about them. If they don't, you can find subtle ways to help them out, like, "I keep bumping my leg on this cool coffee table I built."

With every new project you tackle, you'll connect more deeply with the world around you and build the confidence to try almost anything. That's how it happened for me and all the makers I know.

**SAVE MONEY AND ADD STYLE.** I took a week off to put in a big patio by hand (left). The cat, dog, and I were all pretty happy in the end. Then I dreamed up a cool fence to surround the yard (above). I paid a fence company to place the posts, then I built the sections.

## YOUR GUIDE TO THIS BOOK

This book reflects the whole messy new movement, which includes traditional tools, digital marvels, old-school handcrafts, IKEA hacks, and mashups of all of the above. As a long-time fine woodworker, I love the new freedom. I also love the focus on doing more with less.

Just like the new revolution, this book is crowd-sourced. I traveled the United States to find these makers and projects. In most cases, I visited their work-spaces to photograph the how-to, and when I couldn't get to them, they guided me from afar as I built and shot their projects in my own workshop. One connec-tion led to another, reflecting the generous nature of this warm, passionate community.

My hope is that non-makers will wander through this fun house and see not only what they're miss-ing out on but also how easy it is to join in. If you're already a handcrafter, you can use this book to intro-duce someone else to your world or get inspired to step outside your box and try something new.

Every project in this book is as doable as promised, and you won't need a makerspace to make most of them, just a kitchen table and a few simple supplies. And almost every project is a usable item. It's cool to make a Yoda on your 3-D printer, but I think it's even more meaningful to make the things you use daily. Then you're really part of the solution, pushing back against the powerlessness, making things worth keep-ing, and keeping disposable goods out of the landfill.

Build your world. Self-reliant people have been doing it for millennia.

# AM I A MAKER? A SHORT HISTORY OF A MESSY TERM

The word *maker* has been adopted by a generation to describe almost anyone who designs and makes something independently, by hand or machine or both. But it's a shaky umbrella at best. Here's why.

The maker movement arose in the first decade of the 2000s as an offshoot of hacker culture, which can be traced back to the push for open-source code by the programmers and engineers who invented computers in the first place. So while many of today's makers work traditional materials by hand, the term is still often associated with digital tools and hacks. This is thanks somewhat to *Make:* magazine, which offers projects of all kinds but still has electronics and code at its core. Maker Faires, launched by the magazine in 2006, showcase the movement in major population centers, and the events are still more high-tech than low.

But self-professed makers embrace old-school materials just as readily as new. Millennials adding #makersgonnamake to their Instagram feeds are as likely to be using leather, metal, cloth, paper, or wood as they are high-tech tools. Makerspaces reflect the murky reality. While they offer a chance to use pricey digital fabrication tools, most also include fully outfitted areas for traditional crafts like woodworking, metalwork, printmaking, and more.

*Maker* is also a problematic word for a new generation of highly skilled, professional artisans, who haven't yet found a word that distinguishes them from hobbyists who dabble in multiple modes. On the other hand, this new breed of full-time makers breaks the old boundaries, so terms like *master woodworker* and *welder* don't always apply.

To sidestep the confusion, I called this book *Handmade*, which is a better catchall for what's happening—digital, analog, pro, amateur, and everything in between. I say call yourself whatever you want—just keep making things.

# 2

# building without boundaries

CARDBOARD FURNITURE.
Jonathan Odom built
this surprisingly com-
fortable and durable
lounge chair (p. 28)
from thick cardboard.

**UNENCUMBERED BY** tradition and empowered by technology, today's handcrafters build without boundaries. The projects in this chapter are just three examples—hard to categorize but brimming with joy.

The 2-D patterns for the cardboard chair were created with an easy CAD program, and the construction requires nothing more than a box cutter and a glue gun. The snow sled is an IKEA hack. In this case, IKEA's biggest seller, the Poäng chair, has been completely transformed into a comfortable, stable downhill racer. And the boom box is a mashup—meaning any collision of materials or styles—between a vintage suitcase and a plug-and-play kit of hi-fi audio components.

In the past, outside of art or design schools maybe, none of these projects would have happened. The materials and ideas are too unorthodox, and some of the techniques unheard of. Boom-box maker Ezra Cimino-Hurt found his first set of audio components on the scrap heap in a salvage warehouse for old electronics, and he used them to turn his mp3s into something soulful.

We'll sample some more recognizable crafts soon enough, but for now let's celebrate pure imagination.

# build a boom box from anything

## with Ezra Cimino-Hurt • Ezra Cimino-Hurt is not the first to put hi-fi audio into unusual packages, but he was the first to realize that a vintage suitcase is the perfect container: light and strong, inexpensive, and widely available, with a sense of bygone style that marries perfectly with speaker cones and control panels. There's even a carrying handle included.

**EVERY "CASE" IS UNIQUE.** These are just a few of the hi-fi boom boxes Ezra Cimino-Hurt has made from thrift-store suitcases. They have both battery and AC power, plus Bluetooth capability and standard audio inputs.

While the vintage valise is his calling card, Ezra has put music in all sorts of vessels, from Lucite cubes to huge blocks of glued-up Legos. He has also hosted design competitions for others to do the same. Check out p. 20 for just a taste.

I can't think of a maker who better symbolizes the new handcrafted movement than Ezra, who is putting the soul back into today's mp3 music files, which lack the richness of analog audio or even CDs. Ezra's idea is novel, and his creativity is boundless, but he's as talented and thoughtful as any Old World craftsman. And despite that fact that he sells these boom boxes for a living, he's happy to share what he knows about making them, epitomizing the collaborative spirit of today's makers.

## ANYONE CAN MAKE ONE

Ezra and I considered all sorts of boxes for this build, but we couldn't get away from the classic case. Like everything in this book, this boom box is a project absolutely anyone can build. All you need to find is a sweet suitcase.

The internal components are low profile, so you can choose almost any type of case with a handle—as long as the speakers and controls can go somewhere—everything from a slick, mod aluminum briefcase to a vintage valise like the one I picked out of Ezra's pile. But be patient in your search. "I look for cases that are made with the same care I put into my work," he said. "They really are treasures."

Also, don't go too big for the speakers you're using. You want them to fit nicely on the side of the case, without leaving too much empty space.

As for the electrical components—amp, controls, inputs, speakers, wiring, inputs, and more—you can definitely source those on your own, but the learning curve is a little steep. One more great thing about Ezra is that he sells the same components he uses as boom-box construction kits, in three levels, at very fair prices. Dig around in the store section at caseofbass.com

and you'll find them. We went with the mid-level kit, called "The Thinker," for $200, because that kit and the next one up, "The Royal Box," both add a lithium-ion battery to the AC power port, so you can go cord free, and then just plug in to recharge the battery. All kits include Bluetooth capability as well as a standard auxiliary input for attaching any audio source, like a CD or record player, or your old Sony Walkman.

With the construction kit in hand, you can hit the thrift stores, looking for a case that makes you happy. Ezra says look down and look up, as cases tend to hide in corners and on shelves. Last, while a hard-sided case is easiest to use, a soft-sided case will also work if you reinforce the sides with thin plywood.

If a suitcase isn't your bag, you can make a boom box out of almost anything. Check out caseofbass.com for inspiration.

## helpful tips

The how-to photos on the pages that follow make most of the process clear, but here are a few additional tips.

- The components are pretty self-explanatory. After you place the power pack, screw in the amp/control panel and the aux input, and connect the input selector button. It toggles the amp between Bluetooth and wired input.

  After connecting the speakers to the amp (see p. 24), connect the power pack to the amp and you're ready to audition your case. Usually there will be two problems: interference between the left and right sets of stereo speakers—the left and right channels to be more accurate—plus too much airspace overall, especially in larger cases.

  The solutions are simple, requiring just a few pieces of closed-cell foam and a bit of trial and error. Acoustic or speaker foam is perfect, but upholstery foam is good too.

  Ezra first built a thick divider for the middle of the case, holding off on gluing it in until he had another listen. The sound was much less muddy but still not punchy enough, so he closed off some of the remaining airspace with speaker foam and the sound improved 100%, with thumping base, clear mid-range tones, and a crisp high end.

- Our case didn't rattle when the bass kicked in, but if yours does, try running a bead of silicone caulk between the two halves.

- As for adding personal style to your case—from a speaker cone that's just for looks to anything else you want to stick on—take time to play with the layout. Ezra used tape doughnuts to place stickers in random locations before breaking out the Mod Podge. He also mentioned that the speakers are standard sizes, so you can add covers if you like. He recommends steel grills from Parts Express (parts-express.com).

- And last, a few pro secrets for restoring old cases: Any household cleaner will work for an initial cleanup, with the Magic Eraser doing an incredible

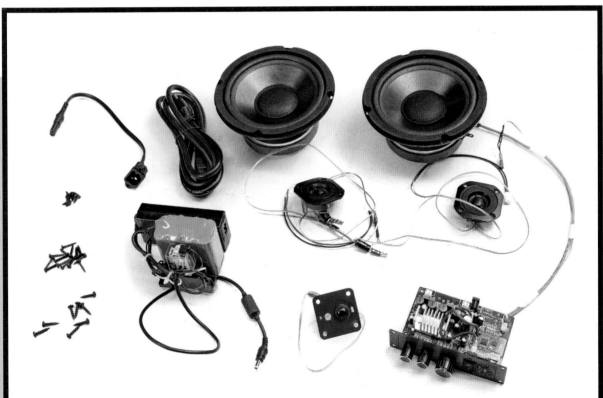

## PLUG AND PLAY

Start with this kit. You can spec the components yourself or buy them in a plug-and-play kit. This Case of Bass kit includes an amp, control panel, Bluetooth connectivity, AC power pack, aux input, four speakers (two woofers, two tweeters), and a rechargeable battery.

"The Thinker" Boom Box
Construction Kit, $200
www.caseofbass.com

job on spots and blemishes. And at the very end, Ezra likes Shape Up, from P&S Sales, a dressing for rubber and leather that sprays on and wipes off, leaving a soft sheen.

Your Case of Bass will look and sound amazing wherever it goes: out and about, in your apartment, or in your workspace, powering you through 100 more maker projects. In every way, it's got soul.

# PUT MUSIC WHEREVER YOU WANT IT

For Design Week Portland in 2013, Case of Bass handed out their component kits and invited designers to build them into innovative packages. This is just a small sample of the amazing results.

Box in a crate.

Ready for vinyl.

**CAN'T BEAT THE CLASSIC.**
The boom box Ezra built for this book is a typical Case of Bass: totally unique and capable of sonic mayhem.

# PREP WORK

**1 STRIP THE LINING.** Pull out all the lining materials, and a hard case is ready to go. If yours is soft sided, you'll need to glue in panels of ⅛-in. plywood using construction adhesive and leave it overnight to dry and harden. This case is from 1949—they don't make 'em like this anymore. **2 CLEAN THE EXTERIOR.** Simple Green will clean off decades of grime without damaging the case, and a Magic Eraser is amazing at removing stubborn spots.

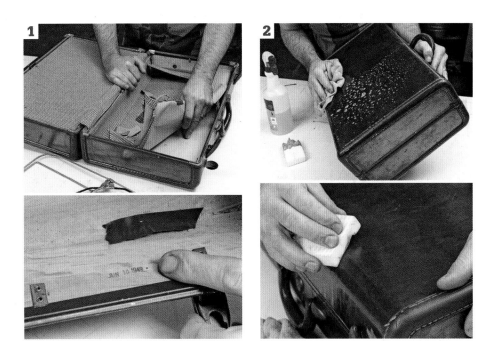

# LAYOUT MATTERS

**1 LOCATE THE SPEAKERS FIRST.** Try them in different spots to find an arrangement that looks just right. You'll need to find a place for the control panel too, but that works best on top of the case near the handle, where it's easy to reach. **2 TAKE A FEW MEASUREMENTS.** Measure from the edges to fine-tune the placement of the big speakers. For the tweeters, try finding the center.

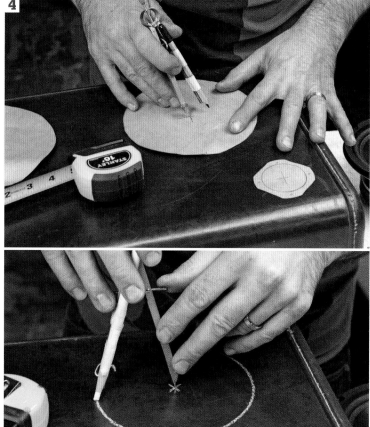

**3 MAKE TEMPLATES.** These reflect the full size of each component and the hole that it requires in the case. Kraft paper works great here, or use a paper grocery bag.  **4 SWITCH TO A COMPASS FOR THE SPEAKERS.** Use the templates to be sure the speakers are evenly placed, and then poke a hole through for the center of each circle. Now set the compass just a hair larger than the hole needed (for the back of the speaker, not the outside!) and draw on the case. A white grease pencil marks better on dark materials.  **5 TRACE THE OTHER OPENINGS.** Trace directly off the other templates for the additional openings needed in the case. Then double-check all your measurements. If something is off, erase and correct it now.

# HOW TO CUT ACCURATE HOLES

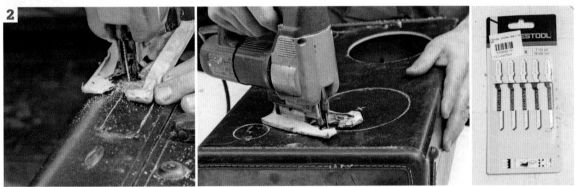

**1 DRILL STARTER HOLES.** Pick a drill bit that's a little bigger than your jigsaw blade, and place the holes just inside the lines.  **2 JIGSAW TIPS.** Use blades designed for scrollsawing (tight turns), like these Festool S50/1.4K blades. A jigsaw will cut every opening you need and nibble them a little wider if something doesn't fit. It's better to creep up on a tight fit than to cut a hole too large.

# ADD THE COMPONENTS

**1 SCREWS NEED PILOT HOLES.** Most of the screws go near the edges of the larger holes, so you'll need to drill pilot holes to be sure the screws don't wander or split the material. Make them a little smaller than the screw diameter. Don't overdrive the screws and strip the holes. By the way, when you attach the woofers, locate their wire terminals near the center of the case.

**2 GLUE IN THE POWER PACK.** Hot glue works well here. The best location is at the bottom of the case toward the center, but try the power cord first to make sure it reaches. Ezra glued down the pack on thin, firm foam, which boosted it up a bit so he could also glue it to the flat bottom of the case at the same time.    **3 EASY CONNECTIONS.** The auxiliary input attaches with a thin nut; the speaker connections are color coded to attach in a series: tweeter to woofer, woofer to amp, on each side (left and right channel separate); and everything else just plugs in.    **4 ALL SYSTEMS GO.** A blue light comes on when you hit the power switch, indicating that Bluetooth is operating, and it turns red when you activate the aux input.

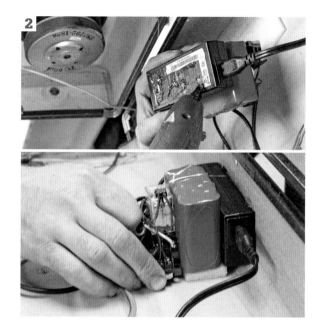

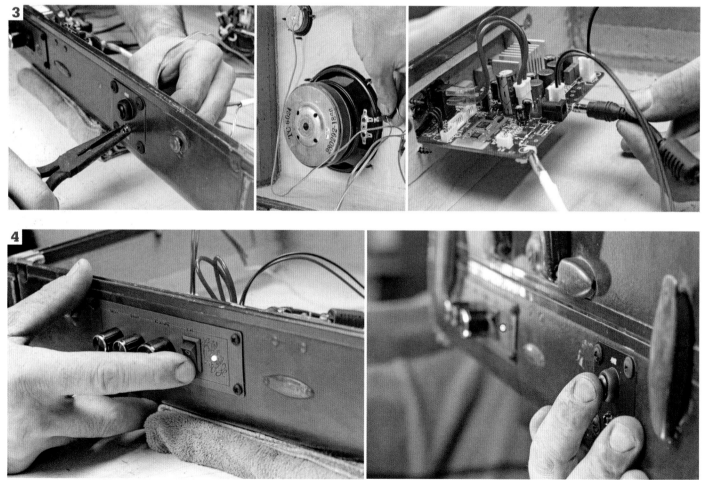

**5 TAME THE WIRES.** Use zip ties to keep the wires together on the right and left side of the case. Clip off the tails of the ties.

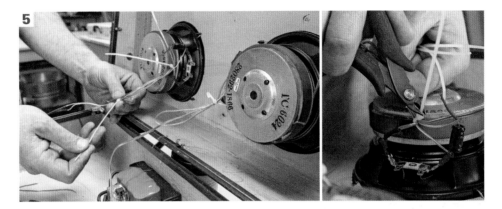

# FINE-TUNE THE ACOUSTICS

**1 TAKE IT FOR A SPIN.** Connect your smartphone via Bluetooth and play some music with a full dynamic range of sound. The sound will probably be a little muddy at this point. **2 DIVIDE THE CHANNELS.** Adding a divider prevents sonic interference between the left and right speakers and greatly improves the sound in most boom boxes. Ezra doubled up pieces of acoustic foam to make his divider, cutting it a little oversize to squeeze into place. Upholstery foam would work, too. Then he put a few extra pieces on both sides of the interior, to close off some excess airspace and make the sound less boomy. The results were amazing.

# PERSONALIZE IT

**1** HAVE MUSIC, WILL TRAVEL. Ezra customizes his cases with all sorts of stuff, including parts harvested from other cases and electronics, but he went for DIY travel stickers this time. He sent images to a local print shop to be output on card stock. Then he rubbed them on the workbench to add some age and applied them with Mod Podge. **2** ONE MORE COAT. A careful coat of Mod Podge on top, only on the stickers, adds some protection. In the end, they look like they've been there for years. **3** ROCK INTO THE FUTURE. Your new boom box is ready to power your maker lifestyle for years to come.

# Ezra Cimino-Hurt

When Ezra Cimino-Hurt was just 13 or 14, his uncle hired him to help frame houses. "I learned how stud spacing relates to the size of sheet goods, the ritual of the lunch break, and how to make a framer's chair," he says, referring to a job-site seat made by cutting up and notching a 2×12. "These guys knew stuff."

His parents, both teachers, sought out jobs at private schools they thought would be right for their four nail-banging, rough-housing boys. "They were hippies in the best sense: kind, intelligent dreamers, and their friends were the same," Ezra says.

The search took the family from middle Tennessee to multiple states, ending in Utah. In 2002, when the Olympic bubble burst in Salt Lake, Ezra followed a friend to Portland, Ore., with his own family in tow. There he balanced construction work with the filmmaking program at the Art Institute of Portland. In retrospect, he was learning the art and storytelling skills he would need to make Case of Bass a success.

Ezra stayed in construction after graduating, starting his own remodeling business, and his brother joined him a year later. Case of Bass was born soon after. "We wanted a better job-site radio, something cooler than the DeWalt," Ezra says. They liked a space-age retro boom box they found at Best Buy, which had exposed speakers, illuminated from inside. "But it was $500, so we decided to make our own."

On a trip to Goodwill, looking for used speakers, they found vintage suitcases instead and had the vessel for their portable stereo.

They got their first parts from a friend's electronics recycling company and soon had three or four marginally working boom boxes.

**WORDS OF WISDOM**

"My goal is to own fewer things that matter more. People think of technology as throwaway. I want to make things that people will cherish and enjoy and will stay functional. If it breaks in five years, I'll fix it. If you wear it out, you've earned that repair! Try fixing things. If you do that enough, you just feel like, 'Let's take this apart.'"

When they brought one to a big Easter brunch, Ezra remembers people saying, "This is the coolest thing I've ever seen. You have to follow this. You have to build these."

The brothers were determined to try, but they needed a name for their business. When Ace of Base came on the radio, "Case of Bass" was obvious. Six years later, Case of Bass is bigger than ever, with Ezra alone at the helm, shipping 150 unique "cases" to clients around the world.

# 2

# make a cardboard chair that really works

**with Jonathan Odom** • It was projects like this innovative lounge chair and the IKEA-hacked snow sled on p. 33 that earned Jonathan Odom a permanent position at Instructables (instructables.com). While hundreds of people contribute to the well-known maker site, only a handful are invited to the Wonka-like factory on San Francisco's Pier 9. Jonathan is joined in this book by Instructables colleague and fellow

**THE REAL DEAL.**
Made from three-ply corrugated box cardboard in just a couple hours, this cardboard chair is comfy and durable.

sorcerer Mike Warren, who contributes IKEA-hacked lights and two concrete wonders in later chapters.

A cardboard chair might seem like a goofy endeavor, but this one is no joke. A conversation starter to be sure and probably not a family heirloom, it's totally functional—both comfortable and durable. In fact, Jonathan had one in his apartment for months, using it daily before recycling it to make room for other maker projects.

With Jonathan's precise templates in hand, you can build this lounge chair in just a few hours, using nothing but a box cutter, a simple straightedge, and a hot-glue gun. Need furniture for your apartment? Get cutting!

## PRINT OUT BIG TEMPLATES

Most adult human bodies—especially the lower half—fall within a narrow range of sizes, so there are established chair dimensions that simply work. To be sure his cardboard chair would be comfy, Jonathan borrowed the seat and back angles from of an iconic lounger—the Barcelona Pavilion chair—and built from there, using Fusion 360, a high-end CAD program. The next step was designing 2-D shapes that would fold and combine to form a 3-D solid, locking together with a series of notches.

Jonathan's Instructables handle is "jon-a-tron." Search that to find the chair project and the three downloadable templates you need, plus 101 other amazing maker projects. Send the template PDFs to a print shop that can output 4-ft. by 4-ft. sheets and have them printed full-scale. If your local print shop can't do it, try a shop that prints construction drawings.

Note that Jonathan has simplified the how-to since the first attempt he chronicled online, so follow the steps in this chapter. For example, he used the

**With Jonathan's precise templates in hand, you can build this lounge chair in just a few hours, using nothing but a box cutter, a simple straightedge, and a hot-glue gun.**

big Instructables laser cutter to speed up the process (you can do the same if you have one of those), but later proved you can do it all with a utility knife or box cutter too.

## THICK CARDBOARD: BUY IT OR MAKE IT

This chair is made from three-ply cardboard, not the single-ply stuff you see every day in box form. Jonathan laminated his own three-ply from single sheets at first, squeezing a mile of squiggly glue lines between the layers and clamping the whole thing down with plywood and weights to get even pressure over as many square inches as possible.

Then he discovered you can buy ready-made three-ply cardboard from companies that sell packing materials, like Uline. The three-ply cardboard comes in a 4-ft. by 8-ft. sheet, which is more than enough for this project. The ready-made stuff will save you time and produce a more solid chair.

If you do glue up your own three-ply, be sure the corrugated lines face the same direction in all three layers, so they fold easily later.

# PRINT AND STICK

**1 DOWNLOAD THESE PDFS.** Go to Jonathan's page on instructables.com (search "jon-a-tron") to find this project and the downloadable templates you need.
**2 PRINT THEM FULL-SCALE.** Jonathan used the large-format printer at Instructables to print out the three pages of templates. You can do the same, inexpensively, at a local print shop. **3 TAPE THEM DOWN.** Cardboard comes in 4-ft. by 8-ft. sheets, plenty big enough for this project. Three-ply cardboard is a must, which you can either glue together yourself from single plies or buy ready-made. Use plenty of tape strips so the paper doesn't come loose as you cut the parts free. **4 PRECUT SOME TEMPLATES.** Precut the templates for the sides so you can flip them around and nest them together on the cardboard without wasting space. Also, note how the big rectangular templates are lined up: Their fold lines are aligned with the corrugated core for easier folding.

5 easy pieces **one awesome chair**

**1**

# Jonathan Odom

Jonathan Odom grew up in rural Louisiana, where his parents home-schooled him through 12th grade. At age 14, he started working at a cousin's electronics factory and stuck with it through college at LSU, where he spent two years in the engineering school before switching to architecture for two more. When the film industry started booming in New Orleans, Jonathan left college to build props. That move led him to Los Angeles and steady work in the movie biz, but he found the culture too slimy and cutthroat for his liking. "Personal conduct is out the window," Jonathan says. "I just didn't want to spend all my time with these people."

That sent him back to architecture school, at SCI-Arc in downtown LA, where he graduated with a bachelor's degree. But the architecture field didn't feel right either.

"I worked for five years in the Bay Area, and hated every minute of it," he says. "I'm a creator at heart—I want to design and invent new things—and you only get to do that at the beginning of a project. The rest is just adapting code regulations and arguing with contractors."

Following his heart again, Jonathan applied for the residency program at Instructables/Autodesk (same company) and got it. After just three weeks in the program, he was hired to create projects and content full-time at the company's idyllic workspace on San Francisco's Pier 9. He loves his job. "You can't hide behind theory and jargon because materials don't lie. You can't fake a good chair." Search his user name, "jon-a-tron," at instructables.com to find step-by-step instructions for his down-to-earth wizardry.

ON THE HANDS-ON LIFE

"If you spend your life trying to get stuff, it becomes very empty. What are you doing with your time? For me, the most authentic life you can have is one where you make things."

KNOW WHAT WOULD BE COOL?

# CUT AND FOLD THE PARTS

**1 CUTTING TIPS.** Use a straightedge to guide your utility knife or box cutter. A 4-ft. aluminum ruler works well, and be sure to use a new blade in your cutter. Try to cut all the way through in one shot, but just make additional passes if you can't. As you cut the notches, fit them onto waste pieces to be sure they are tight, and adjust the other notches as needed. Be aware that some notches will hold two layers of the three-ply cardboard. **2 MAKE PARTIAL CUTS AT THE FOLD LINES.** The templates for the seat, front, and back all include lines where the thick cardboard needs to be folded cleanly. Cut only about halfway through at this point, and cut a bit more later as needed when folding. The goal is to go through two layers but not three!

**3 PREBEND TO GET CLEAN FOLDS.** The precut fold lines go on the inside of the parts. Place your straightedge at the line and bend the cardboard. Cut deeper if it won't fold cleanly, but don't cut all the way through.

# ASSEMBLE AND ENJOY

**1 DO A DRY-FIT FIRST.** Try all the pieces to make sure everything fits well, and then run a thick bead of hot glue along the edges of the sides as you reattach each folded piece, holding each one in place as the glue cools. That will make the chair more solid and durable. You can also run a bead of hot glue along the corners of the finished chair.

# turn an IKEA chair into a sled

**with Jonathan Odom** • Yup, you heard right: We are chopping up an IKEA chair and transforming it into a snow sled—one that will take you down a snowy hill faster than Chevy Chase in *Christmas Vacation*. Jonathan dreamed up this unlikely luge when Instructables (instructables.com) sent its full-time content creators to a cabin in Lake Tahoe to build winter-themed projects. I thought I was lucky to work at *Fine Woodworking* magazine for a few years, but Jonathan hit pay dirt.

**PURE FUN.** This sled looks cool, slides like heck, and attracts attention from everyone on the hill.

Jonathan's first project in Tahoe was a hot tub made from plywood and a tarp, with a portable propane shower heater supplying the hot water; his second project was this one. "I just looked at the Poäng chair and thought, 'I can make this into a sled,'" he says. "So I just figured it out." Not only did he figure it out, but Jonathan's sled uses almost every bit of the chair except for two short arm sections. At $79, the Poäng is one of IKEA's best-selling items of all time—moving 1.5 million units per year—so you might own a couple old ones already.

**SIMPLE SUPPLIES.** You'll need only the frame of a Poäng chair, not the cushions, and just three tools: a small handsaw, a cordless drill, and an adjustable wrench. Plus, of course, that little IKEA hex wrench we all know and love.

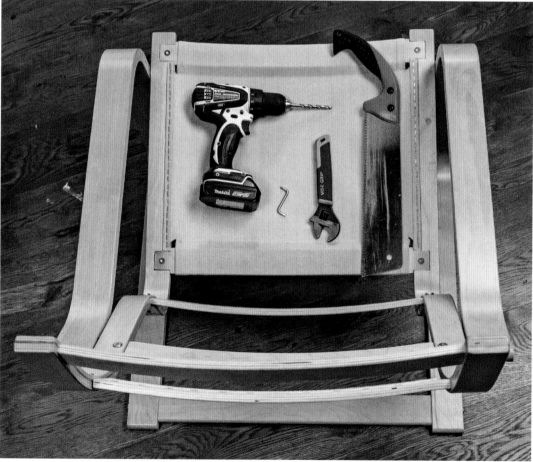

There is real genius in this project, notably how Jonathan uses a combination of straight and curved parts to bolt the seat frame to the skis below, adding butt clearance and springy comfort at the same time. The seat assembly also helps hold the front and back skis together, and the curvy side rails brace the front skis for impact and create handles for the rider.

Most important, the sled works. That was my first question for Jonathan when we connected and started talking projects. He understood the book's practical spirit right away and assured me that the sled is as sweet to ride as it is fun to build.

Just to be sure, I took the sled back with me to Oregon, waxed the runners with an old candle, drove it to the snowy slopes around Mt. Hood, and invited my friends to take it for a spin. It works as great as it looks—light, fast, and comfy. To make it even stronger, replace the drywall screws with nuts and bolts.

As with many projects in the book, you don't need a lot of tools or skills to pull this off. There are only a few cuts to make, which you can do with an inexpensive handsaw. There's a little drilling and screwing after that, and a cordless drill will handle it all. The extra fasteners you need are cheap and simple.

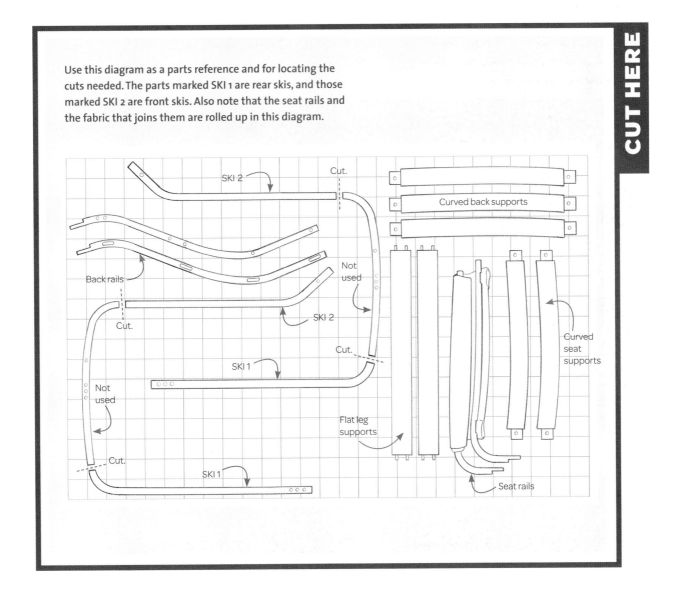

Use this diagram as a parts reference and for locating the cuts needed. The parts marked SKI 1 are rear skis, and those marked SKI 2 are front skis. Also note that the seat rails and the fabric that joins them are rolled up in this diagram.

# CUT AND JOIN THE SKIS

There are two skis on each side of the sled, aligned end to end. Jonathan used an inexpensive handsaw that cuts as you pull it, which is easier to use than a push saw (the traditional type). Check the diagram on p. 35 and mark your starting points. It also helps to mark the entire cut line, square to an edge.

**1 ONE CUT GUIDES THE NEXT.** To ensure matching parts, use one cut part to guide the cuts on the other. Once the cut is established, you can pull the other part away and keep going. **2 FRONT SKIS NEED ANGLED CUTS.** There are two skis on each side of the sled, lined up end to end. To help create a strong joint between the two, recut the ends of the front skis to match the curve of the back skis as closely as possible. This might take some trial and error. **3 JOIN THE SKIS.** Start by drilling pilot holes through both pieces, just smaller than the screws. Then drill slightly larger clearance holes through the top piece, and finally drive in a pair of 1¹/₂-in.-long screws (or 1¹/₄ in., if that's all you can find).

# ATTACH THE SEAT

The seat of the chair is assembled the normal way, with two curved seat supports threaded through the fabric and bolted onto the seat rails. Then Jonathan uses two of the curved back supports, together with the flat leg supports, to attach the seat to the skis below, creating clearance over the snow and adding some spring at the same time.

**1 DRILL MATCHING BOLT HOLES NEAR THE CENTERLINE.** Drill 5/16-in. holes through the back supports (top), and then center these parts under the seat to drill matching holes in the curved seat rails. Center the holes 3 in. or 4 in. apart and place a bolt in one when drilling the second, as shown (bottom). **2 ATTACH THE FRONT SUPPORT.** Attach a curved front seat support and one of the flat leg supports as a unit, using their existing holes and placing them against the front of the rear ski, as shown. Drill pilot holes down into the skis below and then drive 2-in. drywall screws at each end, adding #8 washers. **3 LOCATE THE BACK SUPPORT.** Fit the 1/4-in. bolts into all their holes to position the seat and seat supports, and mark the position of the lower back rail. **4 ATTACH THE BACK SEAT SUPPORT LIKE THE FRONT.** Drill pilot holes down into the rear skis, and then use washers and 2-in. drywall screws to attach both flat and curved back rails as one unit, in the position you marked earlier. **5 BOLT ON THE SEAT.** Use the 1/4-in.-dia., 1 1/4-in.-long, round-head bolts, plus washers and locknuts to attach the seat to the curved seat supports. Use bolts here, not screws, to withstand the stresses at these curve-on-curve junctions.

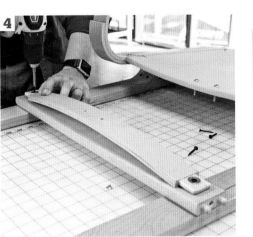

# ADD A FEW BRACES AND ENJOY

The remaining chair parts brace the front and back of the sled and create side handles for the rider. Then it's just wax and ride.

**1 ONE BRACE UP FRONT.** Use 1¼-in. drywall screws to attach one of the remaining curved back supports near the front of the sled, drilling pilot holes first, of course.  **2 ONE BRACE AT THE BACK.** The last curved back support bolts to the back of the seat. To use the stock IKEA bolts and threaded holes, position the curved rail as shown and drill small holes through to the front (left). Then come around with a bigger drill bit to make those holes wide enough for the bolts to pass through, and attach the rail, as shown (right).
**3 TWO FINAL CUTS.** The chair's curvy back rails become side rails on the sled. To keep the tips of the rails from digging into the snow, cut the tips off at an angle as shown, using the cut on one rail to guide you when you cut the other.
**4 PREDRILL THE SIDE RAILS.** Hold them in position as shown, and then drill pilot holes through the slots and into the sides of the seat (left). Now move the side rails and drill those pilot holes deeper in the seat rails (right).

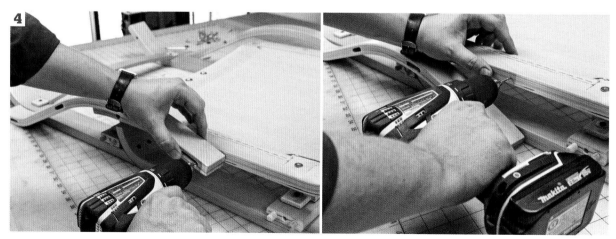

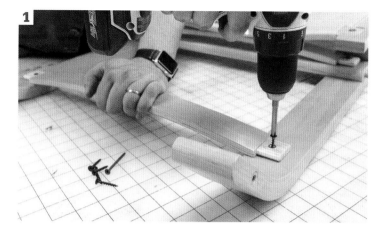

**5 LONG SCREWS.** Use 1⅝-in. or 2-in. drywall screws to attach the side rails to the seat rails, as shown. Then attach the side rails to the front skis the same way.   **6 JUST TWO PIECES LEFT OVER.** Jonathan has only two short arm sections left when he's done.   **7 TRANSFORMED.** The king of the living room is now the king of the mountain. This might be the ultimate IKEA hack.

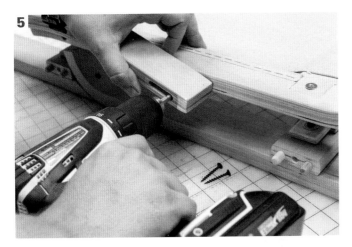

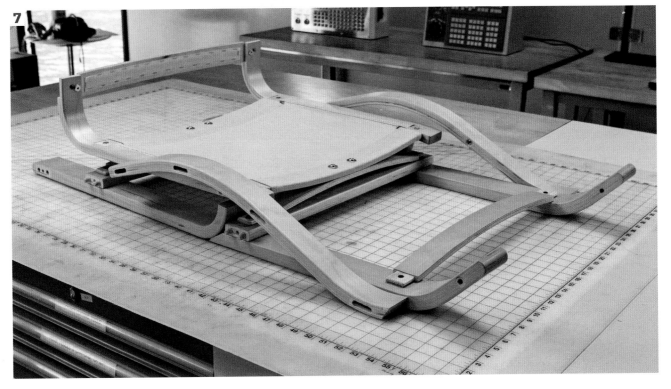

# 3 wood still can't be beat

**THE REASON WOOD** is one of the first chapters in this book is that you just can't beat it as a building material. Widely available in an endless variety of sizes, shapes, and types, from solid lumber to manufactured sheets, wood has an amazing strength-to-weight ratio. It can be cut and shaped with basic tools, and it's just downright pleasing to the senses, with an organic look and feel that's hard to match.

**DOABLE PROJECTS WORTH DOING.**
These easy projects will add handsome handcraftedness to your life and teach you essential skills along the way.

There's just something about wood. Maybe it's the ingenious woodworking techniques that have accumulated over centuries or maybe it's all the wood furniture and wood structures we see all around us, but working wood feels like connecting to history and connecting to nature at the same time.

> **Part of the fun of being a maker is finding great things to build with tools you have—until you're ready for better ones.**

I remember the first time I made shavings and built something from lumber. It was a set of loft beds for my college dorm room, which I made with my dad's old crappy circular saw, electric drill, and beat-up wood chisel. It was a fun engineering problem to solve: deciding how to fit the two college-issue steel bed frames into a single corner unit, how thick and wide the wood pieces needed to be, and how to make a few notches and bolts work together to keep us off the ground and out of the infirmary. I got a little carried away. The loft bed not only made it through my five-year undergrad odyssey but also earned me $50 when I unloaded it on a fellow dorm dweller at the end of my run.

## FIVE PROJECTS TO GET YOU HOOKED

The five projects in this chapter prove that absolutely anyone, using inexpensive materials and basic tools, can make cool projects with wood. These are not your dad's fine oak cabinets and bookshelves. They are innovative projects made from unorthodox sources of wood: reclaimed lumber, deck boards, and discarded chairs given new life.

That said, you'll learn fundamental woodworking techniques in this chapter, which you can apply to more ambitious projects down the road. If you already have some woodworking skills and experience, you'll enjoy a few useful, unique projects that don't take weeks to complete. I've been building fine furniture for years, but I've found new inspiration in things that are fast, fun, and relatively cheap to make.

You'll see a wide variety of tools used in these projects, but most are just suggestions. In other words, there are simpler alternatives, like using a handsaw instead of a power saw. Part of the fun of being a maker is finding great things to build with tools you have—until you're ready for better ones.

Whether you stick with fun woodworking or graduate to fine, you'll pick up some basic know-how in this chapter and maybe become a woodworker for life. I hope you do. To continue your journey, grab a copy of *Build Stuff with Wood* (Taunton, 2017 ). It's a great sequel to the five projects on the following pages.

## BREAKING BOUNDARIES

One of the tricky things about this book is that the projects don't all fit into neat chapters. Take the outdoor tables at the end of this one: They have thick concrete tops, which could easily go in the casting chapter, but the bases teach you how to use a super-valuable woodworking gizmo—the pocket-hole jig—so I put the project here.

In the end, building is building and making is making. Two of my woodworking heroes, Wharton Esherick and George Nakashima, were as innovative with concrete as they were with timber, working a half century ago. Makers gonna make.

PROJECT N°.

# 4 turn a stump into a chair

**with Coby Unger** • Walking past a street-side tree stump and a discarded chair a few houses away, artist friends Coby Unger and Matthew Kramer had a simple thought: "Hey, we could make that stump into a chair." Since then, the two have drilled 30 salvaged chair backs into stumps around New England: in woodsy spots, by commission in public parks, and like the very first stump chair, as a public service

**SERIOUS FUN.** Coby Unger and Matthew Kramer have installed dozens of stump chairs along city streets and in parks and forests. These ad-hoc art projects are part public service, encouraging passersby to slow down and take a seat, and part political statement, intended as a reflection on throwaway culture and the act of making things for oneself.

WOOD STILL CAN'T BE BEAT

in neighborhood stumps—usually embraced by the property owner but occasionally not.

"The goal of StumpChair is to call attention to the lifecycle of a chair while also bringing whimsy to the streets, sidewalks, and parks of the cities we live in. From the beginning, one of our goals was to 'turn eyesores into Windsors,' " Unger said, referring to the ubiquitous stumps and the style of chair he uses most often.

At first Coby stayed anonymous, using a name given to him in a newspaper article, "Johnny Chairseed," but soon he came out as the roving chair installer, publishing photos on his website (cobyunger design.com) and on his StumpChair Facebook page.

While he admits the stump chairs are just plain fun to build, they also make a statement, he says, encouraging others to repair, recycle, and create. "In a world where things are rarely fixed and perfectly usable objects get discarded because they fall out of style, we throw things away without thinking about where 'away' actually is, or what it means."

He adds, "Many people have little knowledge of or experience with building things and rarely think about the source of the objects they depend on in daily life." StumpChair is two artists' answer to what ails us, and Coby and Matthew encourage others to follow in their footsteps.

The New England chairs rarely last more than a few months, Coby says, as spindles break, stumps rot, or folks just break them loose. In the minds of the makers, that only adds to the message. "Natural features are ephemeral and should be enjoyed because of, not in spite of, this fact," Coby says.

Last but not least, Coby says, a chair set in a stump invites passersby to sit, relax, and think—as the boy does in the pages of *The Giving Tree,* Shel Silverstein's classic book for kids of all ages.

I wasn't able to visit Coby in Somerville, Mass., to photograph him at work, so we worked together from a distance as I installed a chair in a friend's backyard and two more in a driftwood log on the Oregon Coast. My thanks to Duane Bolland, who did the marking, drilling, and gluing while I clicked away.

## CHOOSING STUMPS AND CHAIR BACKS

A few caveats before you become the Johnny Chairseed of your neighborhood. For starters, Coby and Matthew do not condone cutting trees to make the stumps you need or taking apart usable chairs. Also, rather than donning your camo and becoming a chair guerrilla, I encourage you to ask property owners for permission. Try showing them a few photos of past chairs and offering to take the chair down if they don't like it.

Another consideration is the condition of the stump itself. Freshly cut is much better than old and rotting. No one wants to sit on an old moldy stump, and the spindles won't stay put anyway. Stump height is another consideration. For the installation pictured on p. 48, Duane first flattened his backyard stump with a chainsaw, establishing the seat height at a comfy 20 in. or so. That said, other heights can work, and a stump chair doesn't have to be perfectly functional to have an impact.

Then there are the chairs themselves. Probably one reason StumpChair started in New England is the abundance of old, traditional chairs you'll find there in various states of disrepair, from ladderbacks to Windsors. There aren't quite as many along the West Coast, but I had no problem finding a broken captain's chair on Craigslist, available for free to anyone who would haul it away. I also bought two beat-up ladderbacks for $5 each from a local staging company that puts on big events.

In both cases, the chairs had problems from the seat down, which only made it easier to remove their backs.

TWO BY THE WATER. Chair backs can go into the side of a tree as easy as a stump, so they work great on downed logs and driftwood, too.

## DIFFERENT WAYS TO ATTACH THEM

While Coby uses yellow glue to install his chair backs, reinforcing them by driving screws diagonally through the base of the spindles, I used two-part epoxy to install mine. Epoxy fills gaps well, maintaining its integrity and grip better than yellow glue in a compromised joint. So I didn't have to worry about the spindles fitting the holes perfectly, and I was able to forgo the screws for a cleaner look. But both ways work just fine.

If you think you or someone else might want to pull the chair out of the stump at some point, just use screws alone. In the end, it's the spirit of StumpChair that counts.

IMPERMANENCE. To make the chair backs easy to remove, install them with screws only, as I did with these two by the sea.

# HARVESTING CHAIR BACKS

Once you find a broken chair, you'll need to separate the back from the seat and legs. Sometimes backs can be simply unscrewed from the chair base. More often they will need to be forcibly removed using a variety of tools—whatever works.

**1 SAW AND SPLIT.** On Windsor and captain-style chairs (like this one), the back spindles need to be freed from the thick seat. Even though this seat was already broken, I needed to do some sawing and splitting to work some of the spindles loose. I made cuts with a jigsaw and then split the seat with a chisel as needed. Afterward I reglued the spindles that had come loose from the curved top rail, using quick-set epoxy for a strong bond. **2 OR JUST SAW.** On ladderback chairs, the back is often easier to remove. On these salvaged convention chairs, I took out the screws that attach the back posts to the seat and then simply sawed through the posts below the seat but above the first stretcher in the base, giving me some extra length to bury in the stump.

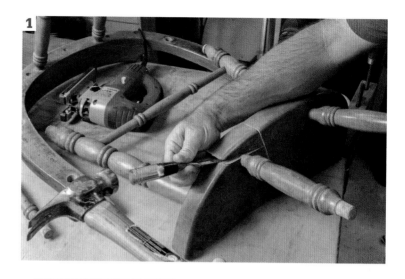

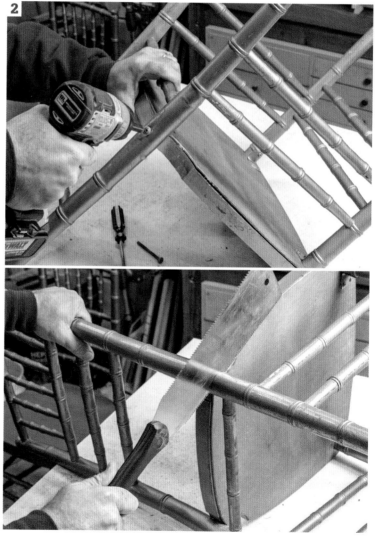

# WHEN SPINDLES BREAK

If you break off the end of a spindle trying to wiggle it free, as I did—twice, you can replace the end with a dowel and proceed as normal.

**1 SAW AND DRILL.** Saw off the broken tip, and then pick a dowel size that is at least ¼ in. smaller than the spindle. It will help you center the big hole for the dowel if you drill a small hole first. Now drill the full-size hole (in this case ½ in. dia.) at least 1 in. deep. **2 INSERT A DOWEL.** Squirt some wood glue in the hole and spread it around with a stick. Then push in the dowel and give it a few twists to finish spreading the glue. After an hour or so, saw it off to about 1½ in. long. The dowel will be just as sound as the original spindle and just a bit narrower.

WOOD STILL CAN'T BE BEAT

# INSTALLING A STUMP CHAIR

All you need for this project is a broken chair, a tree stump, and a tube of epoxy—or screws and glue for a less permanent installation. You'll also need a drill with bits that match the size of your chair-back spindles, and a rubber mallet.

**1 LOCATION AND ORIENTATION.** Look for a flat, non-rotted stump, at a height that is comfortable for sitting. If you have a chainsaw and know how to use it, you can trim the stump as needed. Then decide which way the sitter will face and where the chair back should go.

**2 MARK THE HOLE LOCATIONS.** Make sure the chair back stays in the same position as you mark circles around the spindle tips. A fine-point marker works great.

**3 THE RIGHT HOLES AND THE RIGHT ANGLES.** As you drill each hole, be sure you are using the right-size drill bit (just a hair larger than the spindles is perfect), and keep the chair back nearby so you can match the angle of the chair spindle you are drilling for. Start by drilling straight down in the center of the hole you marked; once the bit gets started, you can tilt it and drill the rest of the hole at the correct angle. Drill farther than you think is necessary. **4. DIFFERENT BITS FOR DIFFERENT HOLES.** For large holes, a Forstner bit works best (left), and for holes ½ in. or smaller, you can use normal drill bits like this one (right).

**5** MIX UP SOME EPOXY. Any quick-set epoxy will work, but look for one with a set time of 10 minutes or more to give you time to get all the spindles driven fully before the epoxy starts to harden. I used 5-minute epoxy, which forced us to move fast. Squirt out plenty of this two-part product (a lot more than you see here) and mix it very well to make sure it catalyzes and will harden fully.   **6** SPREAD THE EPOXY. Use a stick to get epoxy or glue into every hole and to spread it around all the walls. It doesn't hurt to put a little on the tips of the spindles, too.   **7** ALIGN THE SPINDLES AND DRIVE THEM HOME. It will take a bit of fiddling and flexing the spindles to get them all started in their holes, but once you do, a rubber mallet will drive the chair back into place easily. That's all there is to it.   **8** ONE WITH NATURE. I like how the handcrafted wood marries with nature's craftsmanship. Your stump chair won't last forever, but nothing really does.

# Coby Unger

**S**tumpChair is the brainchild of two friends, Coby Unger and Matthew Kramer. I found Coby and his charming chairs on Instructables (instructables.com). Check out his page there for the full range of his wonderful work, with step-by-step instructions.

Like many of the makers in this book, Coby found the courage to follow his own path. Partway through the industrial-design program at Philadelphia University, he realized that the typical product-design job wasn't for him. But he did love his student job as a shop tech. He spent as much time as possible in the wood and metal shops, working on his own projects and assisting others. That's also when he discovered instructables.com and began posting projects on the site. That led to an artist-in-residence position at the Instructables headquarters in San Francisco after he graduated, and a job on the in-house design-studio team. The open-ended nature of his work at Instructables let him explore a wide range of projects and materials, including designing an adaptable and playful prosthetic arm.

After a year in the Bay area, Coby moved to India, where he designed efficient cooking stoves and turned a three-wheeled automobile-rickshaw into a mobile building and learning lab, equipped with four custom folding tables and four toolboxes. Friends there continue to develop curricula around

this platform—on soldering and electronics, basic woodworking, DIY toy making, and collaborative building—for children in orphanages, schools, and community centers.

Since returning to the United States, Coby has been working as a shop manager in the Hobby Shop at MIT, which is open to anyone in the community to build anything they want. Like his shop-tech job in college, Coby's current gig lets him pursue his own creative endeavors while sharing the joy of making things.

# 5

# six-pack caddy
# from pallet wood

**with Asa Christiana** • For decades now, frugal folks have been exhorting us to build projects with pallets. I applaud their passion and pluck, and I love a free stack of boards as much as any other woodworker, but allow me to kick off this project with a caveat. While it's true that pallets are free and widely available—in the biggest cities and smallest towns—pallet wood isn't right for every project.

Pallets are built to be strong and not much else. So the wood is roughsawn, is full of knots and defects, and has varied widths and thicknesses. Wood species—usually red oak or southern yellow pine (a hard softwood)—are chosen for strength over style as well. And last, the pallets you'll find in the free pile have usually been outdoors, with dirt and grease ground in.

All that said, a little brushing and sanding goes a long way, and you can clean up pallet boards for all sorts of rustic projects, like outdoor planters, funky frames, a weathered rack for a row of coat hooks, or the sweet tote in this chapter. The key is to lean into the imperfection, embracing the unique character as part of the appeal.

**PARTY WITH STYLE.**
You'll turn heads when you roll up with this rustic beer (or soda) caddy, packed with a tasty assortment of artisanal libations.

Rustic is the rule. I wouldn't pull a bunch of boards off a pallet, run them through a planer (if you have one), and try to build fine furniture with them. The sand and grit will trash your planer knives, and, in the end, the low-grade wood won't look that great anyway. Embrace the roughsawn, weathered look and let your imagination wander. One of my favorite pallet-wood projects is a stylized flag, with the boards turned into stripes by applying a diluted wash of different paint colors.

One great thing about these rustic projects is you don't have to sweat your mistakes. Feel free to chop up the wood with any type of hand or power saw and call the imperfect cuts and splinters part of the charm. Also, nails look great on pallet projects, and no assembly method is easier than that.

Once you start using pallet wood, you'll notice a difference between the freshly cut ends of the boards and their older surfaces. I don't really mind that disparity, but if it bothers you, just wipe on some stain in a "weathered" color that has brown and gray in it. You can touch up only the fresh-cut areas or wipe a coat over the whole project to bring it all together. Stir the can well, wipe on the stain liberally with a cotton rag, and then wipe off the excess to get the look you want.

## WHERE TO FIND PALLETS

I've driven by lots of "free pallets" signs from coast to coast. For this project, however, I was on a deadline, so I scrolled through Craigslist to see what I could dig up in a day. I found six Portland citizens begging me to haul away their pallet wood, so I dug through the sketchy photos to find the best bets.

Be aware that some pallets will be totally trashed, with only a few scraggly boards still hanging on. On the flip side, there are extra-sweet, nonstandard pallets around too, with better, smoother boards, in sizes other than the usual thick frame pieces and thin slats. Actually, that's what I was looking for on this project: something that would yield a ¾-in.-thick board for the ends of the beer caddy—thick enough to let me nail into them but not so thick they look clunky.

It took some digging and restacking, but near the bottom of the pile at my first stop, there were two winners: a standard pallet with thin slats for the sides of the caddy, and a custom pallet with a semi-clean row of ¾-in. boards on top.

## THE EASY WAY TO HARVEST BOARDS

When you lock horns with your first wood pallet, your inclination will be to start pulling nails and harvesting whole boards. Good luck with that. Aiming for strength at all costs, pallet-makers often use ring-shank nails that are very tough to pull out. I've heard tell of pallets joined with staples, making the boards a cinch to remove, but I haven't found one of those unicorns yet.

This rustic tote is sized to accept all sizes of bottles and cans, from old-school shorties to hip 22-ouncers and even wine bottles. I spaced the slats to show off the labels. Inside is a separate grid made from thin oak slats, which keeps the bottles and cans under control.

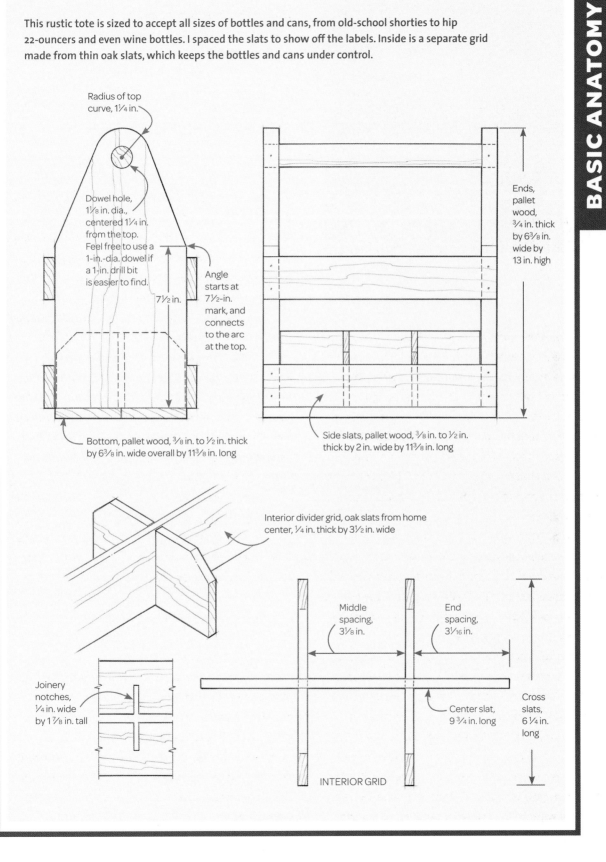

Radius of top curve, 1¼ in.

Dowel hole, 1⅛ in. dia., centered 1¼ in. from the top. Feel free to use a 1-in.-dia. dowel if a 1-in. drill bit is easier to find.

7½ in.

Angle starts at 7½-in. mark, and connects to the arc at the top.

Ends, pallet wood, ¾ in. thick by 6⅜ in. wide by 13 in. high

Bottom, pallet wood, ⅜ in. to ½ in. thick by 6⅜ in. wide overall by 11⅜ in. long

Side slats, pallet wood, ⅜ in. to ½ in. thick by 2 in. wide by 11⅜ in. long

Interior divider grid, oak slats from home center, ¼ in. thick by 3½ in. wide

Joinery notches, ¼ in. wide by 1⅞ in. tall

Middle spacing, 3⅛ in.

End spacing, 3¹⁄₁₆ in.

Center slat, 9¾ in. long

Cross slats, 6¼ in. long

INTERIOR GRID

WOOD STILL CAN'T BE BEAT

**BEST WAY TO BREAK DOWN A PALLET.** It is brutal to pry loose entire boards, though it can be done. If your project allows, use a circular saw to cut the boards loose, running it close to the frame members below. You'll get shorter pieces but will be done in a fraction of the time. Safety glasses are a must here (or your own glasses).

There are a few ways to defeat the nails—just ask Google—but none is fun, and you're likely to split or damage as many boards as you save. If you can avoid pulling nails or pounding boards loose from the back side, I say do it.

My favorite way to harvest pallet wood is the simplest: Run a circular saw along the top of the slats, as close as possible to the frame pieces below, and the slats just drop free. You end up with pretty short pieces, but for projects like this one, those are fine.

If you need your pallet boards full length, there are ways to separate them from the beams below, such as sawing through the nails from the back side, by slipping the blade of a reciprocating saw between the slats and frame. You can also bang the boards loose from the back. I've also seen specially welded prybars custom-made for battling pallets.

## BOTTLE CADDY IS A RUSTIC BEAUTY

This project is so easy to make it could be your very first attempt at woodworking. You'll need a Forstner drill bit or a hole saw to make the holes for the dowel and almost any kind of saw to cut out the pieces; it all goes together with a hammer and nails. Despite the simple tools, materials, and techniques—or maybe because of them—the caddy looks awesome.

Don't feel like you have to use pallet wood for every bit of a project. I wasn't afraid to hit up the home center for the long, thin oak slat I needed to create an internal grid for the bottles and for the thick dowel for the handle. I also added a classic Starr X bottle opener on one end, so I never have to search for one.

**SIMPLE SUPPLIES.** I used one standard pallet (bottom), one nonstandard pallet with ¾-in.-thick boards, a thin oak slat and thick dowel from the home center, a box of 16-gauge by 1-in.-long panel nails (in the "dark oak" color), and a Starr X bottle opener. The cap catcher I'd planned on using was too big for the caddy, so I bagged it. I also skipped the weathered oak stain, once I gave it a try on some scrap.

# ENDS FIRST

The end boards are the foundation. Cut and shape those first, and then the slats just nail on. In fact, you have to lay out only one of the end pieces. After you shape it, you can trace its outline onto the other one.

**1 LOTS OF WAYS TO CUT THESE BOARDS.** I used my miter saw to get a square cut on both ends of a ³/₄-in.-thick board, so I could get both ends of my tote from one board. A jigsaw or handsaw would also work well here.   **2 START BY MARKING THE WIDTH.** Both ends are 6³/₈ in. wide, so I used my combo square to mark that width down the whole board.   **3 CIRCLES ARE NEXT.** After marking where the top ends, 13 in. from the bottom, measure down 1¼ in. from the top and place your compass point there, centered on the width of the workpiece. Set the compass to mark the dowel hole, then set it to 1¼ in. to mark the parallel arc at the top.   **4 NOW THE ANGLED SIDES.** These angles start 7½ in. from the bottom and connect to the arc at the top.

**5 DRILL THE HOLE FIRST.** Clamp the board onto a piece of waste wood, which will prevent splintering on the back side of the hole, and use a big bit to make a hole that matches your dowel diameter. A cheap spade bit will also work, but I went with a smooth-cutting Forstner bit, since I have a nice set of these big-bore specialists. **6 ATTACK THE PERIMETER.** You are cutting off the extra width here as well as the angles and the curve near the top. Two handsaws (backsaw and coping saw) will do the job, as will a bandsaw, but a jigsaw is a cheap, effective option. **7 SANDPAPER DOES THE REST.** Use 80-grit paper, backed with a wood or rubber block, and smooth the curves and angles for a clean finished look. **8 TRACE AND REPEAT.** To lay out the second end of the caddy, just trace the first one onto the other end of your board. Be sure to trace the hole too. Then just drill, saw, and sand this end like the first.

**PRO TIP** Replace your crappy all-purpose jigsaw blades with blades designed for smooth cuts in wood, and you'll be amazed at the results.

# CUT THE REST OF THE PIECES

The side slats, bottom slats, and dowel are all 11³⁄₈ in. long, which makes things easy. I used the miter saw and tablesaw to cut the pieces to length and width, but a jigsaw or handsaw would work just as well.

**1 START WITH THE DOWEL.** Cut one end clean and square, mark the other, and then cut to the mark.
**2 CUT THE SLATS TO LENGTH.** Again, cut a clean end, measure from there, and then cut the other end.
**3 TRIM THEIR WIDTH, TOO.** The side slats need to be trimmed down to 2 in. wide, and at least one of the bottom slats probably needs a trim, too. This is another job where a jigsaw or handsaw would work just fine. The tablesaw just does it quicker. If you do use the tablesaw, be aware that these pieces are not perfectly flat or straight, so use a push stick, like the one shown, to control the boards, keep the splitter in place to prevent kickback, and run the straightest edge of the board against the rip fence.

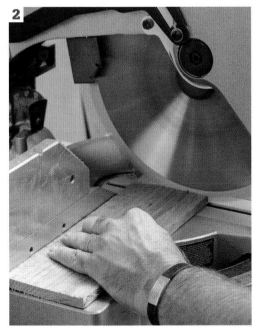

# THE CADDY GOES TOGETHER QUICKLY

After sanding all the boards with 80-grit paper to clean them up a bit without removing the character, start assembling the caddy by nailing the dowel into the end pieces, to help hold them in position as you attach the slats.

**1 DRILL FIRST.** Drill 1/16-in.-dia. holes for the 16-gauge panel nails, through the slats and into the boards below, and they'll go in easy and hold fast. Notice that the dowel is already attached at this point. **2 SIDES THEN BOTTOM.** Nail on the side slats first (left), putting the freshly cut edges toward the bottom and out of sight. Now drill and nail on the bottom slats (right).

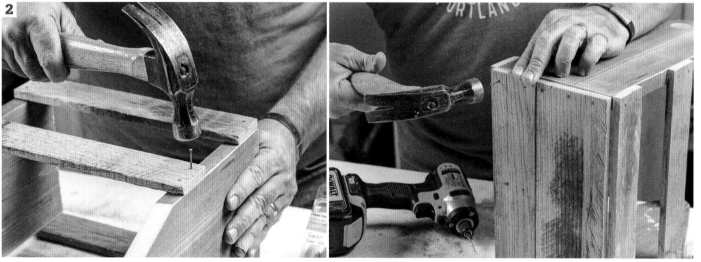

# BUILD THE DIVIDERS

**1**

This separate grid drops into the caddy and sits in the bottom. It's built with mating notches called bridle joints, which are quick and easy to make, and effective.

**1 KNOCK OFF THE CORNERS.** These little chamfers look nice along the sides of the caddy where the dividers show. Again, almost any saw will do, but I used my miter saw. **2 LAYOUT TRICKS.** Start by laying out one side of each notch (left). Then use the mating piece to lay out the other side of each notch, lining it up with the first layout line and tracing the second along the other side with a sharp pencil, so you know the slots will be the right size.

**2**

**3**

**4**

**5**

**3 CUT THE NOTCHES.** A jigsaw or bandsaw works great here. Saw along each side of the notch, using a blade designed for wood, and then nibble away the waste and square off the end of the notch. Last, try to fit the mating piece into the notch you just cut. If it's too tight, take tiny slices off the sides of the notch.    **4 ASSEMBLY SHOULD BE EASY.** Try the assembly first without glue to be sure it comes together and will drop into the caddy once assembled. It's OK to tap on the parts with a hammer and a protective piece of wood to get them to slide home, but if you need to bang on them, you have more work to do with the jigsaw. Now add some yellow glue to the little mating surfaces before sliding the pieces together for the last time.    **5 DROP IT IN AND ADMIRE YOUR HANDIWORK.** The grid just drops into the bottom of the box, where it will sit happily and do its job. Now drop in some bottles and cans and grab an Instagram pic.

# 6 pressed plants in reclaimed-wood frames

**with Glen David McHargue** • With a degree in botany and two generations of woodworkers behind him, it's only natural that Glen McHargue would put beautiful plants into wood frames. The only surprise is how big a hit they were when he put them up for sale. He has made and sold almost 4,000 to date, at retail outlets around Portland and the Pacific Northwest, as well as on Etsy and other sites, helping him launch a part-time woodworking business.

Each one a unique piece of art, Glen's framed botanicals also have a scientific feel, reminiscent of the herbaria that students and collectors once made—lovingly crafted books that preserved and cataloged local flora.

Glen remembers a professor talking about how people see the plants around them as a "green blur" rather than a landscape of individuals. That's partly why he doesn't press and dry rare or flashy plants, but focuses on common local species instead. His goal is to focus the blur, hoping people will "recognize the plants while they are going about their lives."

As a woodworker Glen is just as thoughtful about the frames, which he makes from old boards he finds while working part-time on a construction and remodeling crew. Aside from being free for the taking, much of this old construction lumber came from mature forests in the Pacific Northwest, where it had fierce competition for light and nutrients, making the grain tighter and prettier than the loose-grained wood from today's clear-cut tracts. Age adds a deep patina and rich color. All of the above was true of the strips we sawed off the edge of an old Douglas fir 2×4 in Glen's studio space. Even after we sanded away the dirt and grime, the character of the wood was obvious, especially after a quick coat of oil.

What is especially wonderful about Glen's process is how straightforward it is. After making thousands of these unique works of art and science, he has ironed out all the wrinkles.

## LEARN TO MAKE MITERED FRAMES FROM OLD WOOD

Even if you choose not to fill the frames with plants, this project will teach you how to make mitered frames in all sizes, using any type of wood, reclaimed or new. In fact, some buyers are so happy to find Glen's stylish, distressed-wood frames that they dump the botanical contents to use the frames some other way.

Mitered frames are actually harder to make than they look, with accurate 45° angles to cut and assemble (they become slippery devils when the glue goes on) and a pocket to be cut in the back side that must fit standard sizes of picture-framing glass.

You could buy or cut glass in custom sizes, but glass is pricey. One of Glen's slick tricks is to pull the glass and backer boards from cheap, standard-size frames he finds at the local dollar store. He's got tips and tricks for every stage of the process, and if all you want is frames with character, you can make a stack of them in an hour or less.

## TIPS FOR HARVESTING AND PRESSING PLANTS

Glen cuts only common, native plants that can be pressed flat and will retain their structure and color, like ferns and tree leaves, avoiding most flowers, which are bulky and full of moisture. He also sticks to plants with "secure" status on the NatureServe scale, meaning they are widespread and abundant (see natureserve.org for more info).

As far as when to collect plants, late spring is best, Glen says, after new plants have had a chance to harden and leaves to mature. Soft new leaves dry sort of translucent and fragile, he says, and the color won't survive. Basically, there can't be too much water in the plant, which is why tender, thick, or otherwise water-filled leaves will get moldy or turn brown. You can hang flowers to dry them, but they end up too fat and thick, putting too much distance between the backer and the glass, which doesn't look good.

While he makes and sells simple presses (shown on p. 64) for drying the plants and leaves, you can do just as good a job with an old book. Make it a hardcover for even pressing pressure, and avoid books with glossy, coated paper, which doesn't absorb moisture as well as uncoated, matte paper.

Inside the book you can place fresh plants every four or five pages as you walk the trails looking for

Amur Maple
Acer ginnala
Coll: Glen McHargue #1585
Portland, Ore. 10.10. 2016

SWORD FERN
Polystichum munitum
Coll: Glen McHargue #1309
Portland, Ore. 1.18. 2016

**NATURAL HISTORY.** With regional flora surrounded by wood reclaimed from local homes and buildings, each framed plant reflects history of the place you live. Flat, relatively dry ferns and leaves hold their color and shape well.

handsome plants and colorful leaves. Back home, you should control the drying rate by moving the plants to new pages every day or two as they dry. If they dry too fast, they'll wrinkle and get crispy. Too slow, and they'll get brown areas or grow mold or mildew. But once they are fully dry, the plants can live in the book forever.

Glen also collects root material, which he tries to keep together with small plants, but also sometimes tears away, shakes clean, and dries separately, so he can add it to the bigger plants later.

Once the plants are dry and you have some wood to work with, you'll need only a few power tools to create the frames, along with an air-powered brad nailer for assembly. And if you lack some of these tools, there are workarounds. For those and the rest of the details, follow the step-by-step photos that follow.

# PRESSING PLANTS

You can press and dry plants in a hardcover book or a dedicated plant press. Just change the paper every couple of days as the plants dry, or move them onto new pages. Once they are dry, they can stay in the book forever, waiting to be used.

**1 OLD HARDCOVER BOOKS ARE PERFECT.** Take one with you when you collect plants, and you can press them immediately. Make sure every bit of the plant is lying flat as you close the book. **2 SHAPE PLANTS AS YOU PRESS THEM.** Try pinching one end in the crease between pages while you bend the rest of the plant and close the book. Don't hesitate to use transparent tape to hold plants in position. As they dry, the shape will become permanent. **3 ADD WEIGHTS.** These old-timey irons are cool, but bricks and dumbbell plates work just as well. **4 DIAL IN THE DRYING RATE.** At left are leaves with brown areas and whitish-brown mildew, both the result of plants drying too slowly. At right are ferns that dried too quickly and lost color. **5 TRADITIONAL PLANT PRESS IS FUN TOO.** Glen makes and sells these, but he doesn't mind if you copy his design. It traps layers of plants, paper, and cardboard between simple wood frames, clamped tight with web straps.

WOOD STILL CAN'T BE BEAT

# MITERED FRAMES FROM RECLAIMED WOOD

You'll need a tablesaw to cut strips off the edges of reclaimed boards and notch their inside corners, but you can also use ready-made wood strips from the home center and a handheld router to make the square notches (called rabbets). You can also trade out the air nailer for a simple band clamp, which will hold all four miters together while the glue dries.

**1 RIP OFF THE STRIPS.** Cut strips off both edges of a reclaimed board to create pieces with character on three sides. These are uneven pieces that are a little unstable on the saw, so keep the splitter in place to keep the boards straight and prevent kickback. In our case, we made a short wooden splitter that slips into the blade insert, in line with the back of the blade. Glen also used a push stick to push the end of the board past the blade, keeping his fingers well out of harm's way. **2 TWO SLOTS MAKE ONE RABBET.** The slot will ride right onto the little wood splitter, keeping the board straight as it passes through the blade. The second cut completes the notch (rabbet).

**3 MITER ONE PIECE.** For the two long and two short sides of the frame, start by mitering one piece as shown. Cut one end at 45° (top left), then make a setup block the same size as the frame glass, and drop it in the rabbet to mark the miter at the other end (top right), leaving a little extra wiggle room. Then cut the second miter at the mark.

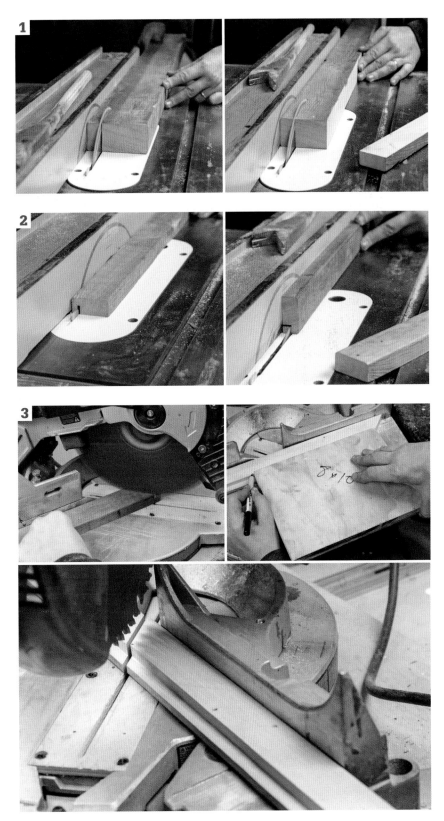

**4 MITER THE MATCHING PIECE.** Here's how to miter a piece that matches the first one exactly. Start by cutting one end of the second piece, and then place the first piece on top of it and line up their cut ends (left). Then lower the blade a bit so you can slide the two pieces over as a group until the other end of the top piece is up against the blade lightly (center). Now remove the top piece without moving the bottom one, and make that second miter cut (right).   **5 ASSEMBLY TRICKS.** Line up all four pieces to wipe wood glue on four miters at once, then do the other end the same way. An air nailer, with 1½-in.-long, 18-gauge brads, is the quickest, easiest way to assemble these miters. Glen attacks the corners one at a time, shooting one nail in one side and two in the other, before moving on to the next joint. Then he wipes off the excess glue.   **6 SAND AWAY THE GRIT AND GRIME.** A random-orbit sander does the job quickly, but hand sanding would also work (back up the paper with a sanding block). Stop when the joints are level and most of the dirt is gone, but don't go much further than that to preserve the age and character of the wood.   **7 APPLY ANY OIL FINISH.** Go for any finish with oil in the title, and wipe on a coat or two to bring out the beauty. The wood will still look old and reclaimed but will be nice and clean.

# Glen David McHargue

Glen McHargue gives his dad the credit for turning him into a DIYer. When he asked for cable TV in his bedroom, his dad said, "Go ahead and do it. Let's figure it out." The same went for rebuilding the furniture in his room. Not every project had his dad's approval though, like the two-story forts Glen built in the woods around Rochester, N.Y., using "borrowed" fence sections nailed to trees. Soon after, Glen started making skateboard ramps, which forced him to build something that was freestanding and structurally sound.

Glen never lost that can-do spirit. In college at Humboldt State in Arcata, Calif., where he earned his bachelor's degree in natural resource management, Glen built loft beds with nothing more than a cordless drill and a tiny cordless circular saw.

During the adventurous life that followed, including contract work studying birds and hawks in Arizona and Oregon, Glen feathered his own nests with better and better furniture. He came to rest in Portland, Ore., working as an arborist for the local utility company.

Today, Glen juggles construction work with his part-time woodworking business, Toadvine. He and his wife live in the old harbormaster's house on a channel of the Columbia River, where they are part of the unique river culture. In exchange for maintenance duties, Glen has the full run of the big workshop next door, owned by a diver who works on floating homes. Glen's wife works with her hands too, at a local shop that sews canvas covers for boats.

**McHARGUE ON THE HANDS-ON LIFE**

"Making things with your hands fills that basic need to provide for yourself and the people closest to you. It just gets contagious and people want to do it more and more. You want to get better at what you're making. Next you start pawning off your stuff to other people to make room for more stuff you want to make!"

# ARRANGING THE PLANTS ON PAPER

Arrange the plants in a clean area, as even one dirty smudge on the paper is obvious. Glen uses white glue to hold the plants in place, which dries translucent and stays a little flexible, and acid-free paper—anywhere between 100 lb. and cardstock, because the glue will wrinkle or dimple anything thinner.

**1 PREVIEW THE DESIGN.** Before moving the dried botanicals out of the book, Glen combines plants and root material and arranges them in a pleasing way, often with inward curves that mirror each other. He often reverses one fern to show the sori, or tiny spore pods on the backside, but he bangs the leaf down a few times to get the spores to drop out, so they don't end up in the bottom of the display area.   **2 GLUE TRICK.** Squirt some white glue in a squiggle on paper and tap the leaf down onto the glue. The idea is to distribute a few dots of glue here and there on the back of the plant without getting any on the front.   **3 PUSH DOWN LIGHTLY.** Put the leaves right where you want them on acid-free paper and push down lightly without moving them. Glen often pauses at this point to weigh down the leaves (see photo 6) to be sure they are fixed in place before moving on to the roots.

**4**

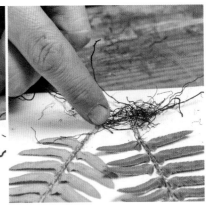

**5**

SWORD FERN
Polystichum munitum
Coll: Glen McHargue #1308
Portland, Ore. 1.18. 2016

**4 REALISTIC ROOTS.** People love to see the whole plant, Glen says. If you can't keep the roots intact as you pull up the plants, here's how to fake it. Start by dribbling on a few dots of glue, and then place some big pieces of root and dribble a bit more glue on top of them. Now grab a little puff of finer roots and place them over the junction of the plant stems and big roots. **5 PLACE THE LABEL.** Glen used to type these out to create an irregular vintage look, but has since discovered a computer font that is indistinguishable from the real thing. The plant is a sword fern, very common in the Pacific Northwest. **6 ADD WEIGHTS.** That same 8×10 setup block goes down to press and hold everything in place. Glen often places wax paper over the gluey spots, so they don't stick to the plywood above, but he used a sticker with a nonstick back this time. Add weights to the top and wait a couple hours for the glue to dry hard and translucent.

**6**

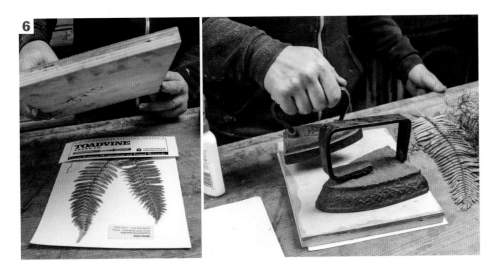

# IT COMES TOGETHER QUICKLY

Once the glue is dry and the plants are fixed on the paper, you can finish the project quickly.

**1 ADD A HANGER.** Glen uses the simple serrated type that simply hammers into place, lining it up by eye. **2 THREE LAYERS.** A piece of glass from a dollar-store frame goes in next, then the paper and plants, and finally the backer board from the same cheap frame. **3 FRAMING POINTS HOLD EVERYTHING IN.** Glen has a special stapler that presses down the contents while driving these flat points into the frame, but there are also cheap framing pliers for the job.

# 7

# DIY doormat

**with Brad Rodriguez** • Just like Instructables (instructables.com), Brad Rodriguez's popular website popped up early and often in my first few Google searches of makers. Launched in 2015, Fix This Build That (fixthisbuildthat.com) has nearly 100K monthly visitors, with an Instagram following of a quarter million at last count.

The projects are designed to be stylish yet doable, and Brad isn't afraid to mix in other materials like concrete, LEDs, and anything else you might find online or at the home center.

I couldn't make it to Tennessee to shoot Brad in action, so we collaborated from afar. I picked out two projects that fit the mission of this book—this doormat and the cool table that follows—and built them in my own shop, with Brad's guidance.

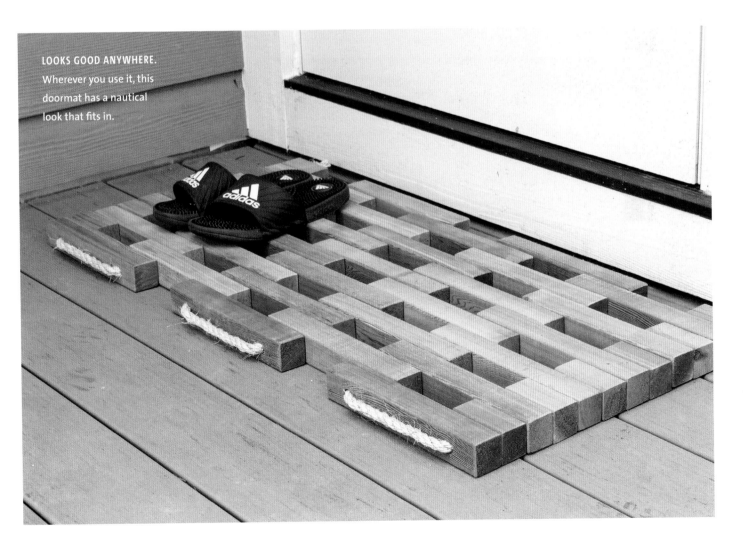

**LOOKS GOOD ANYWHERE.** Wherever you use it, this doormat has a nautical look that fits in.

**SIMPLE SUPPLIES.** You'll need 10 cedar balusters (sold as 2×2s but actually 1½ in. square and each 36 in. long), 15 ft. of ⅜-in.-dia. sisal rope, a drill, and a ⁷⁄₁₆-in. bit, plus any type of saw, hand or power.

It turns out that these two projects are some of the most popular on the site, and it's not hard to see why. Let's start with the doormat, which is one of the easiest projects in this book. It couldn't be prettier or more functional.

## SIMPLE TOOLS AND MATERIALS

I followed Brad's instructions throughout both projects, but added a few of my own twists. In this case, I changed the wood. The doormat requires only a small pile of deck balusters, the long square pieces that go vertically under railings to create a fence of sorts. But instead of the pressure-treated wood Brad used, I went with cedar. Both will stand up to weather and water beautifully, but the pressure-treated wood required a stain to look its best, while the cedar didn't. On the

other hand, cedar is softer and will wear quicker, so you choose. In either case, take your time and pick straight pieces, with as few knots as possible.

I tried to mix things up by trading Brad's sisal rope for some sort of synthetic rope like climbers use (the home center has a long row of choices), but Brad's choice was clearly the best looking.

As for tools, you need nothing more than a handsaw and a drill of some kind. I demonstrate those, but also show how to speed things up with a miter saw and drill press, if you or a friend own those tools.

# START WITH THE WOOD

**1 LOTS OF CUTTING.** You'll need to cut 30 pieces 9¾ in. long and 12 pieces 3 in. long. You can do this by simply marking lines (left) and cutting with a handsaw (right). You should be able to get three long pieces and two short ones from each baluster.

**2 MITER SAW SPEEDS THINGS UP.** Notice the stop I attached to my miter saw by screwing through the back of the fence. That let me cut a pile of matching pieces without measuring. Be sure to hold down the piece that's against the stop as you cut because it's trapped there and could rattle around in an unsafe way otherwise. And don't use the stop trick for the short pieces—it's hard to do safely. **3 MARK FOR DRILLING.** The holes in the short pieces go right in the center, and the ones in the long pieces go 1½ in. from the ends. All of them are centered on the thickness of these 1½-in.-sq. pieces, so ¾ in. from one edge.

**4** DRILLING TRICK. To drill accurately, dimple the wood right at your crisscross marks using a big nail.   **5** TWO WAYS TO DRILL. With a cordless drill, move your head around as you get started to see if you are drilling squarely into the wood. Or use a drill press, which guarantees a straight hole and also lets you set up a fence and stop that will position every part perfectly. In both cases, put a sacrificial piece of wood below the workpiece to prevent chipout at the exit hole.

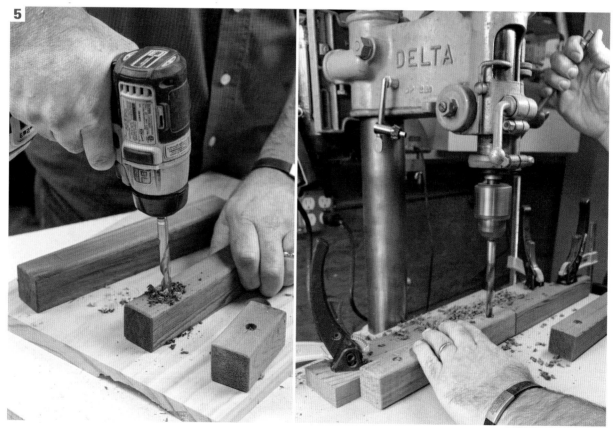

# Brad Rodriguez

**B**rad Rodriguez built his love for working with his hands as a Cub Scout, learning to camp, tie knots, and make Pinewood Derby cars on his way to Eagle Scout. In college, he dove deeper into how things work as a mechanical engineering major and kept the flame alive after he graduated, when he bought a 1905 house in Cincinnati and started fixing it up.

Around the same time, Brad started taking woodworking classes. "I made a simple serving tray and was amazed by what I was able to do with my hands in just one afternoon," he says. "I was loving my newfound hobby and enjoying building things as a creative outlet."

He spent more than a decade working on process improvement and profitability for various companies, renovating another vintage fixer-upper along the way, and learning as much as he could about home repair, woodworking, and everything in between.

Things changed when Brad moved to Nashville in 2013, where he found a vibrant woodworking community. "I poured myself into my woodworking," he says. "I started by building some storage pieces and some shelves for our closet. Then I got into reclaimed wood and made several state signs, some coat racks, and a few other home decor items. I was hooked again!"

Inspired by the responses his projects were getting on Instagram, Brad launched fixthisbuildthat.com in 2015 and a YouTube channel soon after. By 2017 he had so many subscribers, users, and followers (and advertising partners) that he was able to make FTBT his full-time job. "After almost two decades in corporate America, it's so motivating to be in total control of what I do every day and be able to see the direct and immediate fruits of my labor," he says.

Table Saw Cabinet DIY Storage

## ····· ON THE REWARDS OF TEACHING

"I get a ton of emails and comments from new woodworkers and makers. They tell me how my social media, blog, or videos have inspired them to start building and satisfy an urge to work with their hands. They want to see something physical they've made and be able to stand back and say 'I built that!' "

# NOW FOR THE ROPE

**1** **START THREADING.** Wrap tape tightly around the leading end of the rope and work from one end of the doormat to the other, using one continuous piece. Start at the back of the mat, threading the rope through a short piece (I did it wrong here and had to start again!), and then work your way toward the front of the mat, alternating long and short pieces. **2 KEEP ON THREADING.** Tie a knot at the back end and work your way forward to the long piece at the front. Then loop the rope back through the other hole in the front piece and start placing pieces and threading toward the back of the mat. Continue like that, row by row, until you reach the far end of the mat. **3 TIGHTEN THE ROPE AND TIE A KNOT.** Starting at the first end of the mat, start pulling the rope as hard as you can to tighten it and pull the pieces together. Work your way across the mat, pulling the loop front and back, and then tie a tight knot at the far end. Cut off the excess rope and you're done!

PROJECT Nº.

# 2×4 table
# with concrete tops

**with Brad Rodriguez** • Here's another popular project from Fix This Build That (fixthisbuildthat.com), courtesy of Brad Rodriguez. It's a weather-resistant mashup of cedar and concrete, perfect for outdoor use but nice indoors too, where the waterproof top is perfect for plants.

Like the doormat shown in the previous project, I built this table in my garage in Portland, Ore., but I had Brad's excellent online instructions and video to guide me throughout. It was my first time casting concrete for furniture (as opposed to a rough

**2×4 MAGIC.** Made from common materials, this little table is surprisingly pretty and practically weatherproof. The cedar will weather to a silvery color, blending nicely with the concrete.

WOOD STILL CAN'T BE BEAT

concrete step or fence-post footing), so I read his advice carefully and picked up a few pointers elsewhere, too.

Like Brad, I built a pair of these pieces, since two matching side tables look better than one. This is the most ambitious project in this chapter, but that means you'll learn even more valuable lessons.

> **This is a great project for getting your feet wet in concrete, figuratively that is.**

## LEARN A SIMPLE, STRONG WAY TO JOIN WOOD PIECES

With its cool concrete top, this table could have easily gone in the chapter on casting, but there's a lot of wood here and a cool little jig every wannabe woodworker should know about.

Not long after you start trying to build stuff with wood, you'll encounter a basic problem: how to join parts solidly at right angles. Most projects depend on that fundamental joint. There are wonderful traditional methods, like dovetails and tenons, but those have a steep learning curve and require serious tools. Then there are wood screws. Those are easy to use, but often not strong enough on their own. That's because they go into the end grain of one of the pieces you are joining, and screws just don't hold that well that way.

Enter pocket screws. Inserted at an angle, they cut across the grain of both pieces for a really strong grip. They are called pocket screws because they are buried in long holes (pocket holes). These do show on the finished project, but you can usually orient them so they are out of view.

What makes it all work, and makes it so easy, is a little gizmo called a pocket-hole jig. The best are made by Kreg and are available with various levels of features. Like Brad, I used the $40 entry-level version that you simply clamp to your workpieces. It is just as effective as the fancier models and works for wood up to $1\frac{1}{2}$ in. thick. The $40 kit comes with the stepped drill bit you need as well as an assortment of screws designed for the job.

Read the instructions carefully, use the jig as directed, and just a few screws will make a surprisingly powerful connection between any two pieces of wood or plywood, letting you build cabinets, furniture, and a host of other projects.

As for the connection between the concrete tops and wood bases, that's even easier. A few dabs of silicone caulk provide a soft landing and a strong grip.

## LEARN CONCRETE CASTING, TOO

This is a great project for getting your feet wet in concrete, figuratively that is. Concrete is an amazing medium for making things. The two concrete projects in the casting chapter show off even more of its boundless potential.

I have plans to cast my own concrete kitchen countertops at some point, and these tabletops are a mini-version of those, with a similar flat form and a closely related process. The nice thing with these small slabs is that the tops need no internal reinforcement. But Brad's longer coffee table version does: a thick wire mesh buried halfway through the thickness. Bear that requirement in mind if you attempt to make bigger tabletops, or countertops for that matter. On its own, concrete is self-supporting only for short distances, but it's amazing how a little steel inside makes it strong enough for the tallest buildings and longest bridges.

The key to this form and many others is that you are casting the tabletops upside down. That's because

**SIMPLE TOOLS AND SUPPLIES.** To make two tables, you'll need (clockwise from top left) two 60-lb. bags of high-strength concrete, four 2×4 cedar boards (8 ft. long), a few long clamps, a cordless drill, a circular saw, a carpenter's square, a pocket-hole kit and a box of 2½-in. pocket-hole screws, plastic feet, silicone caulk, and a 2×4 sheet of melamine particleboard (seen on the bottom of the pile). A tablesaw is also very helpful for making the concrete form, though you can get by with the circular saw.

it's easier to control the surface that's against the form than the open surface on top. What's cool is how you can round the top corners of your finished table-top by putting silicone caulk in the bottom corners of the form.

Other than the upside-down thinking, the other key is making the form from materials that won't stick to the concrete. Silicone caulk won't, nor will the slick melamine particleboard Brad and I used to make our forms. Other ways to get the concrete to release after it cures are putting packing tape on the form or smearing on a special compound designed for the job.

If you really want to be efficient, you could build the form and cast the concrete first, giving it a few days to harden while you build the bases. But I wanted to build the wood bases first, just to be sure of their finished dimensions before sizing the concrete form to match perfectly.

## AVOIDING WORM HOLES

One common problem with concrete castings is bubbles and worm holes left in the mix, often at the surface where they end up very visible. There are a number of ways to prevent these. To start with, use your hands to press the concrete into all the corners as you go. Concrete is very drying to the skin, so wear some sort of plastic or rubber gloves, or wash and moisturize your hands immediately after. Then, as you start to fill up the form, lift it and let it slam down a few times. And last, when the form is full, you need to vibrate it. You can do this with all sorts of vibrating power tools: sanders, multitools, or a reciprocating saw (without the blade in it). They key is to vibrate the form all along its outside surfaces. A lot of bubbles will rise and pop at first. Stop vibrating when the bubbles are few and far between or you'll risk overvibrating and creating more of them.

If, despite your best efforts, you get lots of holes in your tops, don't panic. If you have a few, just patch them as demonstrated in this project. If you have a lot, you can buy a skim coat product and fill all the holes in one go, leaving a nice smooth surface.

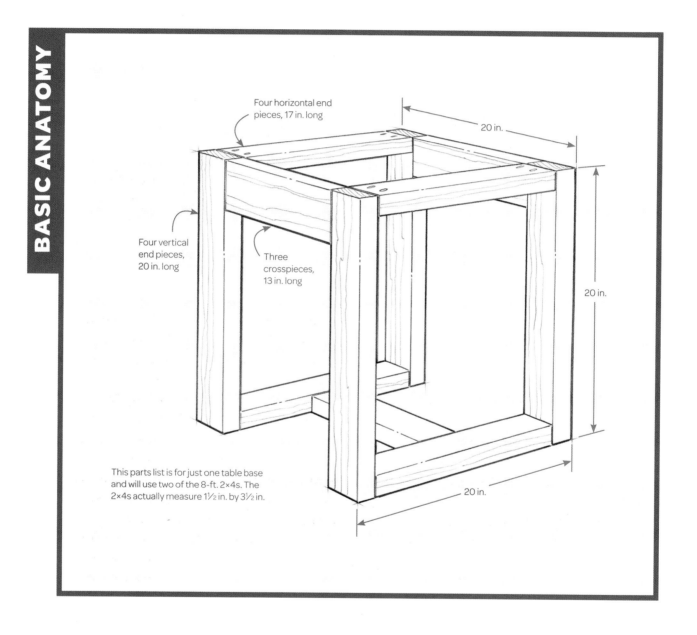

Four horizontal end pieces, 17 in. long

Four vertical end pieces, 20 in. long

Three crosspieces, 13 in. long

20 in.

20 in.

20 in.

This parts list is for just one table base and will use two of the 8-ft. 2×4s. The 2×4s actually measure 1½ in. by 3½ in.

**CUT THE PARTS TO LENGTH.** There are lots of ways to do this, but one of the simplest is to mark a line and use a carpenter's square and circular saw, as shown.

# A FEW MORE PRO TIPS

You can make this entire project with a circular saw and cordless drill, though a tablesaw will be very helpful for making the form, as you'll see. To cut the particleboard pieces to size using the circ saw, clamp a straight board (fence) to the workpiece to guide the base of the saw. A straight 2×4 will work. To figure out how much to offset the fence away from the cut, you'll need to measure from the left side of your saw's base to the blade.

Also, your 2×4s will look just fine if you choose good ones from the pile at the home center or lumber-yard. If you have access to a planer, though, you can skim a little off each side of each board to clean them up and get rid of some of that big roundover on each edge. But don't take off too much wood, just 1/16 in. at the most.

The great thing about cedar is how nicely it stands up to the elements. But there is one caveat. When you pick through the pile, avoid cedar boards with creamy-white streaks in them. That's sapwood, from the outside of the log, and it will rot outdoors in a couple of years. Also, cedar will weather to a lovely silvery-gray, which will look nice with the concrete, so you don't have to bother putting a stain or finish on it.

And last, the pocket-hole jig works great, but there are a couple of potential pitfalls. For one, I noticed the stop collar came loose after a while, causing me to drill too deep. Tighten it after every few holes. If the stop collar fails altogether, you can just draw with a Sharpie on the shank of the drill bit so you know where to stop. Also, it's easy to overdrive the screws, sending the sharp tip out the far side, where people will see it and could cut themselves. Try to prevent that, but if it happens, stop there and use a metal file to level the sharp tip with the wood. If you just back out the screw a little, you'll have a weak joint. Another option is to back out the pocket screw all the way and replace it with a slightly fatter, slightly shorter screw. Just stop at the right point this time!

# POCKET-SCREW JOINERY IS EASY AND EFFECTIVE ━━

I used an affordable pocket-hole kit from Kreg to build this table base. Here are a few important tips for great results.

**1 GET SET.** The jig has a sliding stop (the gray part) for the thickness of the material you're joining, 1½ in. in this case. You'll also need to position the stop collar correctly on the drill bit; flip the jig over and there is a guide for that, too. Be sure the little setscrew on the stop collar is tight and check it periodically as you work. **2 CLAMP AND DRILL.** The gray stop will place the jig the right distance from the end of the board. To position it consistently side to side, I just lined up the edge of the gray part with the edge of the board and used the outside hole in the guide. You'll need only two pocket screws to join each board, so just do the same thing near the other edge. Stop drilling when the stop collar hits the jig. **3 CLAMP AND DRIVE.** Be sure to clamp the workpieces in the precise position you want before driving pocket screws. Otherwise, the diagonal screw will tend to pull the parts out of alignment. Use screws designed for pocket-hole joinery and choose the right ones for the materials at hand (2½-in.-long screws for 1½-in.-thick stock in this case). Drive each screw until you feel it hit the bottom of the pocket hole and pull the parts together. The long driver bit I'm using here also came with the pocket-hole kit.

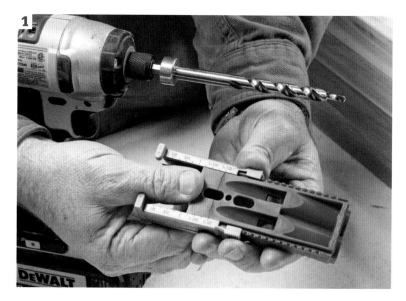

# ASSEMBLE THE BASE

Once all of the pocket holes are drilled, assembly goes quickly. Just be sure to clamp each part tightly in position before driving screws.

**1 HIDE THE HOLES.** Pocket screws leave big unsightly holes in the wood, but it's not hard to hide them on many projects. For example, on the top of this base (left), the holes will be hidden by the concrete tabletop. Others face the floor (right), and none is visible as you walk around the finished table. **2 ADD FEET.** The table will be a lot steadier if you add feet to the bottom boards. These little plastic ones just screw on.

# BUILD THE CONCRETE FORM

Measure your finished table bases and size your concrete form accordingly. The form makes both tabletops at once, which is nice. I used my tablesaw to cut out the pieces, but a circular saw would work too, with some kind of straightedge clamped on the workpiece to guide the saw (see p. 81)

**1 TABLESAW MAKES IT EASY.** Start by cutting out the big bottom of the form, which is the exact size of the two tabletops plus the center strip that divides them. Then cut the sidepieces to length and width. **2 PREDRILL THE PIECES.** Draw a line to indicate the center of the panel you'll be screwing into, and drill holes big enough to let the screws pass through without touching. Notice that I ran out of particleboard for making the form, so I just used standard plywood, covering it with packing tape to make it nonstick.

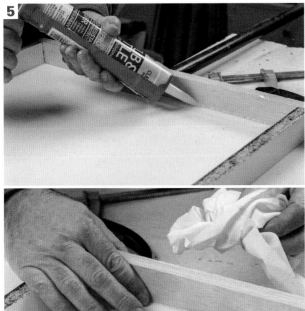

**3 CLAMP, DRILL, AND DRIVE.** If you have long clamps, it helps a lot to clamp the parts in place before driving the screws. Also, be sure to use a drill bit smaller than the screws to reach through the bigger holes and drill pilot holes in the edges of the big base panel. Otherwise, the screws will split the particleboard.    **4 ADD THE CENTER DIVIDER.** The form gets a center divider, which creates the two separate tabletops. Cut it so it fits snugly end to end and ends up level with the top of the form. Then measure and mark lines at the center of the form and drill clearance holes for the screws. Finally, clamp the divider in place and drive screws to attach it.

**5 ROUND THE CORNERS.** Remember that the tabletops will be cast upside down in the form. To create nice round edges on them, squirt a thin bead of silicone caulk into all corners of the form and smooth it with your fingertip, wiping off the excess onto a paper towel.

# CONCRETE CASTING: KEYS TO SUCCESS

Once you add water, you have about 30 minutes to get the job done, so here's how to keep things moving and ensure success.

**1 MIX A LITTLE AT A TIME.** Pour about half a bag of concrete mix into your wheelbarrow or mixing tub and start adding water in small amounts, stirring and blending the mix as you go. Once you get this first pile to the consistency of peanut butter, start adding more concrete and water (sparingly), maintaining that consistency as you empty the first bag. **2 START FILLING THE FORM.** Shovel the concrete into the form, pat it down with the shovel, and start mixing more as needed. You'll need to mix about a half bag more to fill the form. Along the way, use one hand to push the concrete into all the corners, and try raising the form and letting it slam down. (I wear a glove on the hand I use to push the concrete into the form.)

**3** **EMBRACE THE SCREED.** A screed is nothing more than a straight board, a little wider than the form. Use its edge and flat face to work the concrete back and forth, skimming off the excess and creating a smooth surface. **4 GOOD VIBRATIONS.** To release air bubbles from the mix, which will end up on the visible edges of the finished tabletops, you need to vibrate the form. There are dedicated power tools for this, but a recip saw (shown here) also works well. Remove the blade, place the tool against the form all along the side edges and bottom, and vibrate for 10 seconds or 20 seconds in each spot. Bubbles will rise and pop.

# TOP OFF YOUR TABLES

It takes concrete up to 30 days to dry and cure completely, but you can take it out of the form and use it after just a few days. Finishing and attaching the tops is easy.

**1 FORM COMES OFF EASILY.** Unscrew the side pieces and pull them away from the concrete. Both the melamine surfaces and packing tape should come away easily. Then you can just slide the tabletops off the form.    **2 PATCHING HOLES.** You are likely to have a few bubbles and worm holes still on the surface. If they are big and unsightly, you can patch them with the same concrete mix. Sift out the larger sand and gravel first and add water sparingly to create that peanut-butter consistency. Then smear the mix into the holes and level it with your finger. Give it a day to dry and sand it level.

**3**

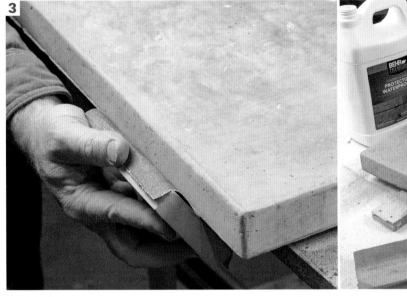

**4**

**3 SAND AND SEAL.** Concrete sands easily with normal paper and a block. Use a rough grit like 60 or 80 to round the lower corners of the tops and higher grits to polish and reshape other areas. Then wipe on a concrete sealer to protect your tops. Keep flooding it on until the concrete won't soak up anymore, and then wipe off the excess. **4 POP ON THE TOPS.** Put a generous blob of silicone caulk at each corner of the base, but not too close to the edges. Then lower the tops into place, sliding them around to make them even on the bases. Leave them right there for a day while the silicone dries, and then your tables are ready for action.

# 4

## learn to work leather

**EVERYDAY ITEMS THAT EXUDE QUALITY.** A valet, belt, and key-loop lanyard are classic accessories you will use every day, and the handsome bridle leather will get only better looking with age and handling.

**AS GEOFF AND VALERIE** Franklin say at the beginning of their *Idiot's Guide: Leather Crafts*—a book that's way too smart to have stupid in the title—"Leather can be considered mankind's first fabric." Ancient societies depended on leather for survival, using various compounds and solutions, including saliva, to break down the protein structures in the stiff, dry hides and make them less susceptible to decomposing.

Tanning technology has moved on (thank science), and today all sorts of leathers are widely available. Like wood, leather only gains character and soul as you use it, but it has some distinct advantages over the splintery stuff. Being thinner and more flexible, leather is easier to cut, shape, and stitch together with inexpensive hand tools.

For all of these reasons, leather is more popular than ever, with a new wave of makers using it to craft everyday items that exude quality yet are unmistakably handmade.

**BONUS PROJECTS.**
Use your leftover leather
and new tools to make a pile
of zipper pulls, which add a
touch of style and function to
jackets, backpacks, and more.

## YOU'RE IN GOOD HANDS

I had a few other leather makers in mind for this chapter, but my good friend Matt Preston, of the ADX in Portland (see pp. 10–12 for more on ADX and other makerspaces around the country), sent me directly to Geoff and Val Franklin. They call their workshop Walnut Studiolo and call the beautiful little coastal town of Nehalem, Ore., their home. For more on the amazing things they make, see the sidebar on p. 104.

Geoff handles most of the making for Walnut Studiolo. Like all the best makers and teachers, he can clarify his techniques simply because he knows them deeply. Beware of "experts" who hide behind jargon and make you feel more intimidated than empowered.

Just like he and Val did for *Idiot's Guide*, Geoff picked the perfect projects for this chapter: totally doable and totally worth doing. The valet is a shallow leather tray for small items, like everything you carry in your pockets and need to carry out the door—keys, phone, wallet. It could just as easily hold jewelry. The key-loop lanyard will lock onto a belt loop or backpack,

adding style and security. And last, there is a classic flat leather belt with top-quality hardware, an essential accessory that can be sized and styled any way you like.

Geoff understood the book's mission completely, trading some of his higher-end pro tools for the simpler ones he started out with. In fact, you can do every project in this chapter, plus many more, with roughly $65 in hand tools. But before we dive in and start cutting and building, let's talk about leather. It varies by source, tanning process, and intended use, and it's really cool.

## A BUYER'S GUIDE TO LEATHER

Straight off the animal, a hide is stiff and unusable. The tanning process involves removing the hair, breaking down proteins in the skin to make it pliable, and replacing volatile oils with more stable ones to create an amazing natural product that will breathe, flex, protect, form to fit your body, look better with age, and last a lifetime with a bit of care.

If you are worried about the moral implications of using animal hides, realize that the vast majority of leather—certainly all of the cowhide we are using here—is from hides left over from food production, material that would be wasted otherwise. As Geoff and others point out, leathercraft is a way to honor the whole animal.

There are two basic tanning methods. The faster process, invented during the Industrial Revolution, employs chromium and mercury to produce very soft garment leathers, used in shoes, purses, and clothing. It's a cheaper, quicker process than older methods and produces leather that can take bright colors in every hue. The other most common process is vegetable tanning, which is used for thicker leathers used for belts, bags, bridles, and the like.

Vegetable tanning has been around from the beginning. The active ingredients are wood tannins, which are what originally gave the tanning its name. This type of leather requires use and handling to look and feel its best, and additional treatments with dyes, oils, and waxes to resist water. That said, vegetable tanning is much more environmentally friendly than chrome tanning, and vegetable-tanned leather smells and looks more natural.

We'll use a type of vegetable-tanned cowhide called bridle leather for all the projects in this chapter, and it's a great one to pick for future projects, too. Bridle leather comes in a range of rich browns, impregnated with waxes and oils so it looks and feels great on both sides, resists water and weather, and might last as long as you do.

A good source for leather and tools is Tandy Leather (tandyleather.com), which has been supporting leathercrafters for decades; eBay is an even better place to find deals on small pieces, which you can use for everything here but the belt.

When you start shopping for leather, you'll be asked what part of the hide you want. It's a reminder that you are buying part of an animal. The key-loop lanyard and valet can come from smaller sections, like a shoulder, but for the long belt (unless you buy a precut version), you'll probably need to buy a half hide, which is split down the center of the back. That's the only way to get the long, consistently thick pieces you'll require. You might be able to get two belts from every full-length strip you cut, so hold on to that hide and you'll get another 16 or 20 belts from it, one for every friend and family member who wants one, plus a range of other projects. Stop cutting belts when you get near the belly, which is too flexible and stretchy.

Thickness matters, too. The belt obviously needs to be thick and stout, but the valet is made from thinner bridle leather, still thick enough to hold its shape, but not so stiff that it needs to be grooved with a gouge along the fold lines. See the individual project info for the thicknesses you'll need for each.

**SIMPLE TOOL KIT.** You can make everything in this chapter with (clockwise): an X-Acto knife ($4), a No. 2 edge beveler ($14), a ruler ($1), a strap cutter ($25, manufactured by The Leather Works and available from various sellers), a rotary hole punch ($15), and a snap setter and anvil ($7).

# 9

# tabletop valet

### with Geoff Franklin ● This
shallow leather tray teaches basic leather
skills, including cutting, punching holes,
and installing snaps, and holds your
essentials in style.

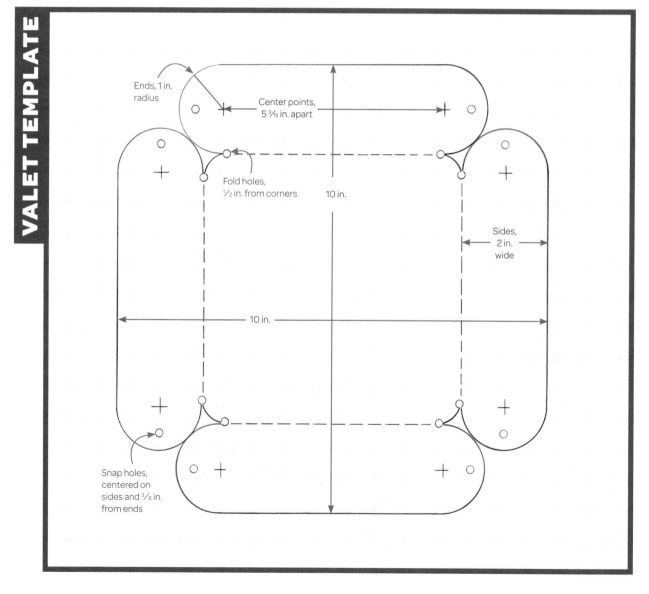

Ends, 1 in.
radius

Center points,
5 ³⁄₁₆ in. apart

Fold holes,
½ in. from corners

10 in.

Sides,
2 in.
wide

10 in.

Snap holes,
centered on
sides and ³⁄₈ in.
from ends

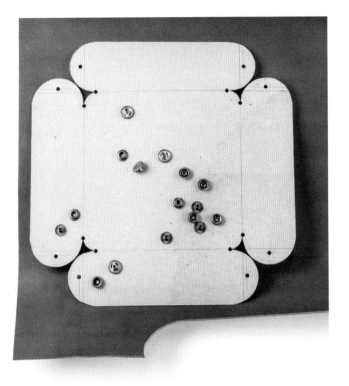

**MATERIALS NEEDED.**
You'll need a piece of dark brown, 2-oz. to 3-oz. bridle leather and four line-20 (aka 20 line) snaps, plus a template cut out of thick paper or thin cardboard (the kind used to make shoeboxes).

# CUT OUT THE SHAPE

**1 TRACE THE TEMPLATE.** It helps to clamp the template on the leather so it doesn't move. Use a sharp pencil or a mechanical one. Don't forget to trace the holes too.
**2 STRAIGHT LINES FIRST.** Lay a metal ruler flat against the leather and use an X-Acto knife with a fresh blade. You should be able to cut through this thickness of leather in one pass with a sharp blade, but don't feel bad if you can't. You'll sense it when the blade cuts through. **3 PUNCH HOLES NEXT.** These will give you a place to stop when you are cutting the curves. Fold the leather as needed to reach the inner holes, and use the No. 2 punch on your rotary hole punch to make ⅛-in. holes. **4 NOW CUT THE CURVES.** Once again, a very firm hand should get you through the leather in one pass. Note how the holes make a clean starting or ending point.

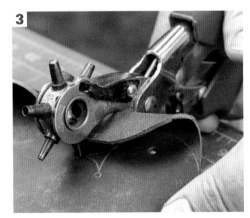

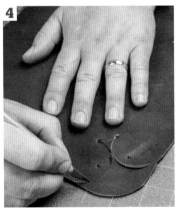

# ADD THE SNAPS TO FINISH THE BOX

1 **LINE-20 SNAPS.** These snaps have four parts, two for each side. They are handsome and easy to install, and they hold fast. 2 **INSTALL THE STUD SIDE.** After you put the post through the hole and the snap, lay it down on a flat, hard surface and hammer the snap setter firmly to peen the end of the post and join the two parts permanently. 3 **CAP SIDE NEEDS PROTECTION.** The cap goes on a small curved anvil to protect it when you pound on the snap setter. 4 **SNAP AND FOLD.** Fold up each side to join the snaps at all four corners and then crease the edges to refine the shape of the box. Note how the holes and cutouts at the corners let the sides fold cleanly.

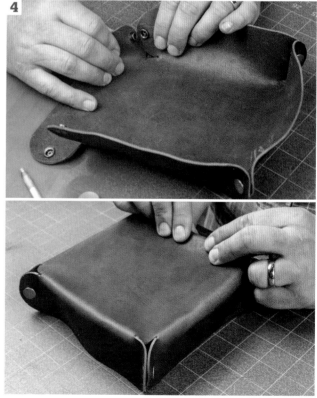

# 10

# key loop with brass hardware

**with Geoff Franklin** • This simple snap loop with quality hardware will keep your keys secure in a pocket or backpack. Other than the trigger-snap hardware, the materials, tools, and techniques are the same as for Project No. 9.

## KEY-LOOP TEMPLATE

The width is sized to fit into the swivel trigger clip, and the length is enough to hang off a belt and drop the key ring safely into your pocket.

³/₄ in.  ◄─ 2 in. ─►  ◄─────── 8 ³/₈ in. ───────►

◄──────────── 9 ³/₈ in. ────────────►

**MATERIALS NEEDED.** You'll need more of the 2-oz. to 3-oz. bridle leather, one more line-20 snap, plus a swivel trigger clip with a D-ring sized for a ¾-in.-wide band, and another cardboard template.

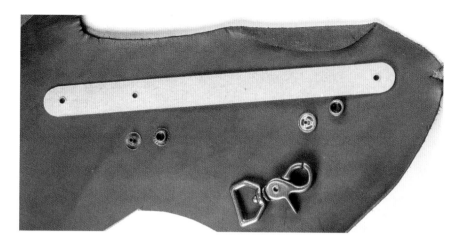

# CUT, TRACE, AND PUNCH

**1 CUT ONE EDGE THEN TRACE.** Establish a straight edge first, and then hold the template against that edge to trace the rest of the shape and the hole locations. **2 FINISH CUTTING OUT THE STRAP.** Fit an X-Acto knife with a fresh blade, and you should be able to cut through this leather in one pass, as you did for the tabletop valet. **3 PUNCH HOLES AS BEFORE.** Use the ⅛-in. (No. 2) size on the rotary hole punch (see p. 95).

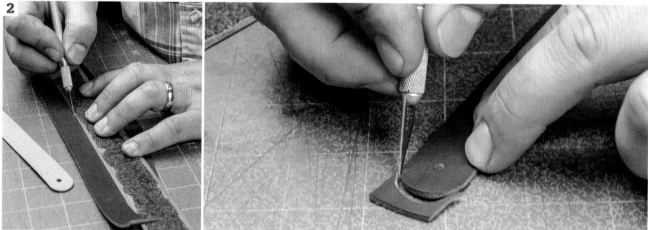

# THIS SNAP HAS A TWIST

In this case, the stud part of the snap goes through two layers of leather to create a permanent loop around the key-ring hardware, while the cap side goes through the long end of the strap, so you can loop it around your belt as needed.

**1 INSTALL THE STUD.** You'll need at least 1 mm of the post to protrude at the top to peen it over properly, so you might need to hold the loop down firmly and hammer a little harder to get this part of the snap set. Also, be sure to add the swivel clip before setting this snap! **2 ATTACH THE CAP AND YOU'RE DONE.** Use the little anvil to avoid marring or denting the cap (left), and then close the snap to finish the project (right).

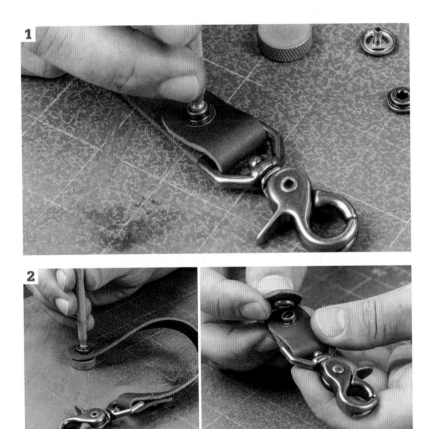

# build a belt and a few new skills

### with Geoff Franklin

A belt is the most useful item of all and will introduce you to new hardware, thicker leather, and a couple of cool new tools. This belt's width and buckle size are standard for menswear, but narrower and wider buckles are widely available.

## BELT TEMPLATES

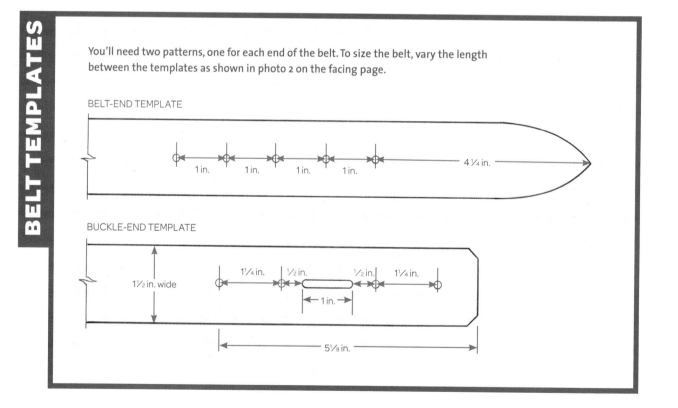

You'll need two patterns, one for each end of the belt. To size the belt, vary the length between the templates as shown in photo 2 on the facing page.

BELT-END TEMPLATE

1 in.   1 in.   1 in.   1 in.   4 ¼ in.

BUCKLE-END TEMPLATE

1 ½ in. wide

1 ¼ in.   ½ in.   ½ in.   1 ¼ in.

1 in.

5 ⅛ in.

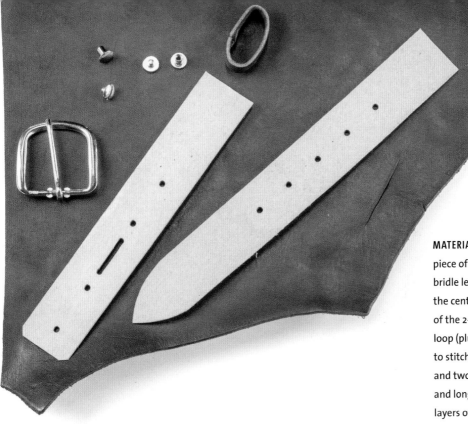

**MATERIALS NEEDED.** You'll need a long piece of 8-oz. to 9-oz., dark brown bridle leather, taken from an area near the centerline of the hide; a small bit of the 2-oz. to 3-oz. stuff for the belt loop (plus some waxed nylon or sinew to stitch it shut); a 1½-in. belt buckle, and two Chicago screws (⅜-in. size and long enough to reach through two layers of leather); plus two templates.

# CUT THE BELT TO SIZE

The thick leather is cut down the centerline of the hide for consistency in look and thickness, as close to the top of the back as possible.

**1 STRAP CUTTER NEEDS A STRAIGHT EDGE.** This tool is a wonderful addition to your growing collection, but it needs to have a straight edge to ride on. So start by using a long straightedge and your X-Acto knife to establish the first edge of the belt. Before using the strap cutter, it helps to clamp down the strip you are cutting at some point. **2 SIZE YOUR BELT.** To start, choose the best-looking part of the strip for the pointy end of the belt. Then position the two templates with the desired waist measurement stretching from the center hole on the pointy end to the farthest hole on the buckle template. Now trace both templates and all of the slots and holes.

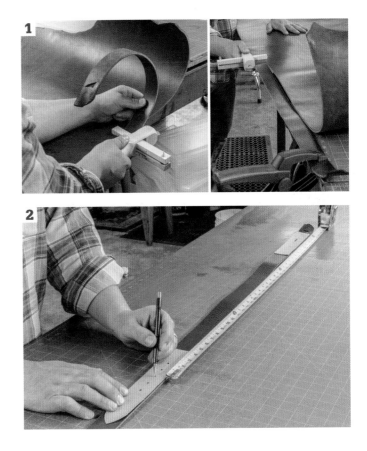

**3**

**4**

**5**

**3 CUT THE ENDS.** Again, use a fresh X-Acto blade, but this time start with a light pass and then increasingly firm ones to get through this thick bridle leather. Don't forget to cut the little corners off the buckle end.

**4 CONNECT HOLES TO MAKE A SLOT.** All of the holes are made with the no. 5 punch, which is roughly ¼ in. dia. To form the slot, punch holes at the ends and connect them with straight cuts.   **5 FINISHED EDGES.** You can skip this step, but rounded edges give a belt a finished look and feel. Geoff prefers the Weaver brand of edger, in the no. 2 size. The trick with this tool is getting the angle of attack just right, which is about 45° in both directions, vertical and horizontal.

LEARN TO WORK LEATHER

**6**

**6 BUILD THE BELT LOOP.** Cut this loop from the thinner (2-oz. to 3-oz.) bridle leather, punch a small hole in each end, and stitch the ends together with three loops of waxed twine, with a square knot on the inside. The wax makes the string more durable and waterproof and keeps it from untying. **7 ATTACH THE BUCKLE WITH CHICAGO SCREWS.** These are handsome and secure but also reversible if you ever want to replace the buckle, which is likely to wear out before the belt does.

> **PRO TIP** A dab of Loctite Threadlocker or latex paint on the tip of the screws keeps them from working loose.

**7**

# Geoff Franklin

G eoff Franklin's love for leathercraft began in 2009, when his daily bike commute sent him searching for accessories with style and function, like classic leather bar wraps. In modern photos of vintage Italian bicycles, he saw many more leather accents that had only improved with age. He taught himself basic leather techniques and began making some of these items, as well as some total originals too. Facing the recession and a tough job outlook, his wife, Valerie, put a few of Geoff's items on Etsy (etsy.com) and discovered they had hit on something big. Soon his southeast Portland garage housed a full-time business they dubbed Walnut Studiolo, with Geoff focused on the leather work and Valerie running the business side. When Portland's rising rental prices drove them out of town, they followed their hearts and kept driving until they reached the Oregon coast, where they purchased a lovely property with a house and a big pole barn. The barn houses everything they need to make and ship 4,000 items a year to customers worldwide.

**WALNUT STUDIOLO.** Geoff Franklin's products include beautiful bike accessories and a wide range of other items, from drawing tubes to leather zipper pulls.

# light up
# your life

**FEARLESS FIXTURES.**
Like many makers,
Jedden White uses
a wide array of
materials and cool
bulbs to create
unique lights.

**HANDCRAFTED LIGHTING** is one of
the easiest ways to add charm and personality to
your living space. Easy to make and hard to miss—
that's the killer combo.

Powering this trend is a host of newly available
supplies, which makes it easy to put lights into
almost anything—and anywhere. Once-hard-to-
find components are just a few clicks away, and new
items like LED strips and Edison bulbs only expand
the possibilities.

Spend a few minutes on Pinterest or Houzz (houzz.com) and you'll find more ideas than you can handle: handmade wall sconces, Mason jars and kitchen colanders upcycled as pendant lights, skateboards with light bulbs for wheels, horns and driftwood wrapped with strings of tiny LEDs, and too much more to list here.

## LIGHTS MASH UP WITH ANY MATERIAL

The coolest thing about DIY lights is how the electrical components can be combined with almost any other material. Wood is an awesome vehicle for lighting designs because it can be shaped, drilled, and crafted so many ways. The same goes for found objects and building supplies from the local home center—almost all of the materials in this book in fact. Whatever

you're good at, whatever you're into can be the basis for heavenly light.

To get you started on the path to illumination, the makers in this chapter present two common types of DIY lighting—table lights and pendants—the first completely handmade, the other made by upcycling IKEA products. Just for fun, I'm throwing in one more popular pendant: Mason-jar lights, which add homespun charm to any food-prep or eating area.

You'll learn all the key details in the project write-ups that follow, including important safety tips, letting you create lighting designs that are all your own.

Almost anything can become a light. The fish (above) and steel-pipe array (pp. 107 and 108) are from the mind of Jeddin White, and the wood pendant light was crafted by Kayla Burke of Portland, Ore.

# 12

# make a tabletop light with copper pipe

**with Jeddin White** • This light is DIY from the ground up, made with traditional lamp components and copper plumbing pipe. If you want to lock in the design, you can glue the pipe joints. But if you don't, the joints can be twisted and reconfigured to change the entire shape of the lamp.

**A VERSATILE MEDIUM.** You can cut and configure the pipe any way you like. For a design like this one, you probably want to glue the joints and make the shape permanent.

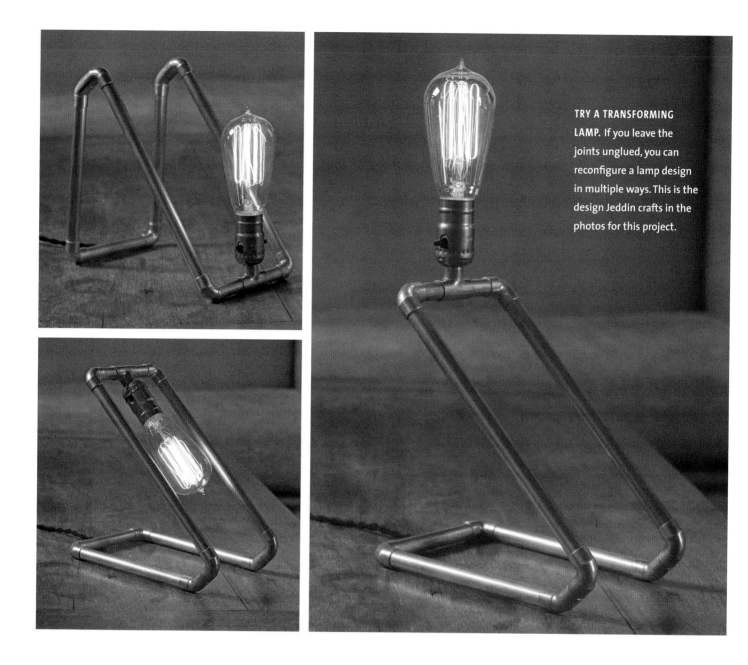

**TRY A TRANSFORMING LAMP.** If you leave the joints unglued, you can reconfigure a lamp design in multiple ways. This is the design Jeddin crafts in the photos for this project.

An eye-catching Edison bulb is the other star of the show. With elaborate, glowing filaments, these beautiful bulbs hark back to an earlier age, when you could see exactly how things worked just by looking at them. And they are dimmable, so you can put them on full display, using them without a shade, as Jeddin does here. Once available online only, Edison bulbs are now sold at your local home center or hardware store in all sorts of glass and filament shapes, with many more available online and at specialty lighting shops. Longer-lasting LED filaments are also available.

The Edison's steampunk style matches the copper pipe beautifully in this project, but it looks great with lots of other materials, too, from plumbing pipes to finely crafted wood bases.

All the how-to is detailed in the photos, except for one part: Jeddin strongly recommends making a drawing to preview and refine your lamp design, once you know the size of your bulb and socket.

**SIMPLE SUPPLIES.** You'll need copper plumbing pipe and joints, a bottle of metal polish like Brasso, a wire with a plug and dimmer switch, a lamp socket that fits loosely in the pipe, and some sort of craft cement or epoxy for gluing the socket into place. You'll also need a few simple tools, seen in the how-to photos that follow.

**EDISON'S MAGICAL DISCOVERY.** Edison bulbs recall the very first electric lights. Their elaborate filaments are fully dimmable, letting you toggle them from a soft glow to a bright blaze.

# CUT AND DRILL THE PARTS

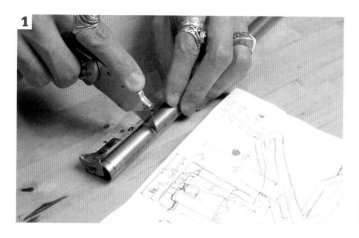

**1 MARK THE LENGTHS.** Working from your drawing, use a tape measure and knife to mark the pipe for cutting. **2 A PIPE CUTTER IS CHEAP AND EFFECTIVE.** This Tarvol mini-pipe cutter is $10 on Amazon (amazon.com) and handles pipe between ⅛ in. and ⅞ in. dia. Clamp it onto the pipe and twist it to start making a groove. Just keep tightening the cutter and twisting it until the pipe is cut. **3 DRILL THE BASE PIPE.** The cord will thread down from the lamp socket, through the pipes, and out a hole in the base. Drill that hole now. The key is starting with a small bit and stepping up gradually to the 5/16-in.-dia. hole you'll need. Feel free to hold the pipe in a vise, but be sure to protect the soft copper from metal jaws.

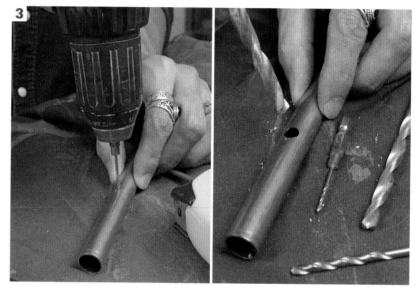

# POLISH AND PAINT

**1 PREP THE PIPES.** Peel the stickers off the pipe and use Goo Gone to remove the adhesive. Then polish with Brasso to get rid of the dirt, marks, and tarnish, leaving the copper bright and shiny. **2 PAINT THE SOCKET TO MATCH.** It's hard to find copper-colored lamp sockets, but a quick paint job creates a perfect match with the pipe.

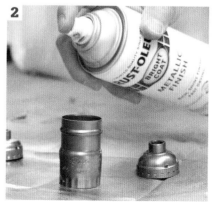

# Jeddin White

After earning a degree in psychology, Jeddin White tried his hand at lab work, running experiments for grad students and analyzing data. After a couple of years, frustrated by months-long studies with inconclusive results, he headed back to his hometown in Iowa and went to work for a construction contractor. Around the same time, he inherited a house that needed work. He gained hands-on building skills and felt a newfound sense of satisfaction. "I was able to finish what I started," Jeddin says.

The next stop on his maker journey was a job at the Floating Bed, a company that hangs custom beds from a single point. That job taught him how to work with rope, fabric, steel, and many other materials. About that time, Jeddin went to Burning Man for the first time, an annual gathering in the Nevada desert where artists build an interactive city, live in it for nine days, and then remove it without leaving a trace. He met a lot of fellow makers there, along with people from the film industry in Los Angeles.

With a job offer to dress the set of an independent movie, Jeddin headed to LA and has lived there ever since, heading out to Burning Man every year, where he now runs one of the themed camps that make up the temporary city. The movie industry is a challenging one, with 12-hour days and lots of time spent looking for the next gig, so Jeddin looks forward to Burning Man as a chance to live an entirely different life. The hat he is wearing in the photo is one he made for the 2017 event, along with a gas-powered DIY scooter.

**WHY BURNING MAN MATTERS**

"A lot of the art is participatory, and that had a huge impact on why I like to build things. One of my main motivations is when I show something to people and they get that moment of awe, when they are wide-eyed, like 'This is so cool!' That's what I live for. And then it inspires them to go and make cool stuff, too."

# ASSEMBLE THE LAMP

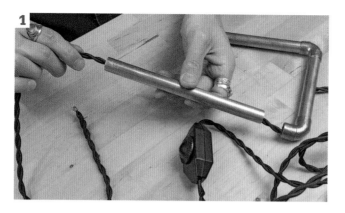

**1** WIRE THE LAMP AS YOU BUILD IT. Insert the wire in the hole you drilled in the base, and then thread it toward the socket as you add joints and pipe sections. **2** ATTACH THE SOCKET. Once the base is assembled, thread the cord through the base of the socket and attach the wires to the screw terminals. Then attach the upper part of the socket, locking it into its base. **3** GLUE THE SOCKET IN PLACE. The base of the socket fits loosely in the top of this T joint, but a bead of E6000 craft adhesive will hold it in place nicely. The E6000 also works well for gluing joints. Apply the adhesive to the base of the socket, then pull apart one of the nearby joints to draw the wire tight and the socket downward while the glue dries. Leave it overnight for full strength. **4** PLUG AND PLAY! Jeddin chose a nice big Edison bulb for this transforming lamp. Avoid leaving fingerprints on the bulb. They create hot spots, which can cause the glass to break. Feel free to give the whole lamp a final polish with Brasso.

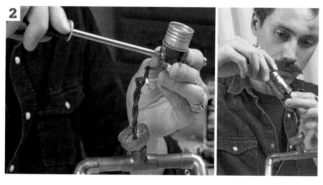

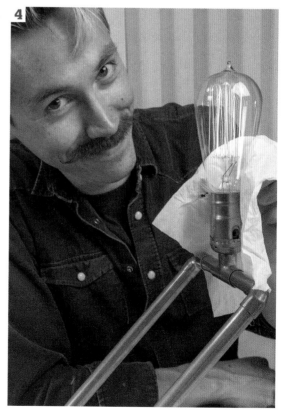

# 13

# hack IKEA for cool pendant lights

**with Mike Warren** • Mike Warren is the second full-time Instructables (instructables.com) employee featured in this book, joining Jonathan Odom of Chapter 2 fame. They landed their coveted gigs by being extraordinary inventors, as comfortable with digital tools as with traditional crafts. Both are adept at making amazing things with very simple supplies.

You'll find Mike's genius all over instructables.com and in three places in this book: here and in Chapter 6, where Mike works little miracles with a bag of concrete. To find out more about Mike Warren, check out his maker story on p. 115.

Mike's inventive pendant lights are IKEA hacks. For a variety of reasons, IKEA is fertile ground for subversive DIYers. For one, most items are sold as separate components that you assemble according to those iconic instruction sheets—or not. Second, the components are both inexpensive and

**UPCYCLING IS FUN.**
The two colanders will work great in a kitchen or eating area, but the sleek steel wastebasket shade can go anywhere.

nicely designed in a clean, modern way. So they blend well with other materials and designs.

If you're looking for strips and strings of LEDs, funky bulb bases with switchable wires, and all sorts of ways to suspend those components in midair, IKEA is worth a long stroll. I walk through IKEA the same way I wander the home center, imagining unintended uses for the endless array of strange and wonderful supplies. With a stop for meatballs and gravy, I tend to wander even farther at IKEA.

Warren's two pendant lights, as well as my Mason jar lights that follow, make use of the wiring IKEA sells for their own line of pendant lights and shades. There are versions with switches and plugs attached and versions without, in case you want to wire them directly into an outlet box for a cleaner look (consult an electrician friend for that).

Mike and I both went for the wires with switches and plugs, which means you'll have at least one wire running across the ceiling and down the wall, depending on how many lights you combine and how you combine them. But the wires are cool looking, so they add to the overall style.

**GOOD IN GROUPS.** You'll need to sort out a way to combine the cords, as with the round plywood disk I used here, but DIY lights look extra-great in groups. By the way, IKEA sells a triple-pendant cord set that's all ready to go. For lights placed farther apart, another option would be to hard-wire each cord into a separate box in the ceiling, all switched at the wall.

The other cool thing about these IKEA bulb bases is how they will clamp solidly around almost any thin material, if you drill the right-size hole in it. That lets you turn almost anything into an awesome lampshade, like two kitchen colanders and a small stainless-steel wastebasket.

**SIMPLE SUPPLIES.** All you need to create lights like these are the IKEA cord sets, a cordless drill with a 1¾-in. hole saw (make sure it has "bimetal" teeth for cutting metal), and whatever you can upcycle as lampshades. Mike got the small stainless-steel wastebasket and both colanders at IKEA, too.

# Mike Warren

**M**ike grew up in Vancouver, B.C., where he earned his bachelor's degree in applied science, focusing on architecture and construction engineering. After college, he stayed in Vancouver, working for the city planning department, evaluating building proposals. Frustrated by the slow pace of development projects, Mike spent his free time developing his own creative ideas, which had a quicker payoff. "I was basically dreaming up things that didn't exist, but should exist." One early project was the "Hand Sandwich," with bread shaped like a hand so the fingers become finger food, literally. Another was dinosaur heels for his wife—shoes with a reptile pattern on them and dinosaurs in the heels. "Now there are heels like that," Mike says.

His friends didn't make much of anything, so Mike found his community online. He started posting projects on Instructables (instructables.com; search "mikeasaurus") and was soon tapped to monitor comments and forums. After attending a 2010 Maker Faire near the Instructables headquarters in San Francisco, he decided to take an internship position at the company. After just two weeks, Instructables asked him to come aboard full-time, and he has been there ever since.

**ON THE TERM *MAKER***

"People sometimes think if you are a maker, you're a hobbyist, like you are goofing around. Words like *craftsman* imply that there is a deliberate process for creating an item—like an Artisan or an Artist with a capital *A*. There is a level of credibility that comes with those terms, but they don't exactly fit what I do. The real word is *inventor*, but people say what have you invented? If it isn't the lightbulb or vacuum cleaner or anything they've heard of, they discredit you right away."

# SIMPLE HOW-TO

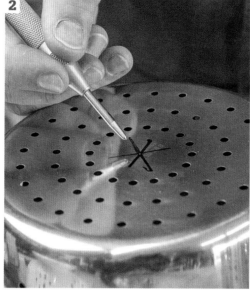

**1 FIND THE CENTER.** Mike combined a framing square and carpenter's speed square as shown to make intersecting marks at the center of these big round objects. **2 DIMPLE YOUR MARK.** A small indentation, made with a spring-loaded center punch like this or a hammer and nail, will keep the drill bit on the hole saw from wandering. **3 EASY DOES IT WITH THE HOLE SAW.** The hole saw has a drill bit that goes through the metal first to keep it on track. It helps if you lubricate the saw with a little oil. Press lightly on the drill, especially when it's about to break through the other side. It tends to grab at that moment. **4 ATTACHING THE LAMP BASE IS EASY.** A little screw-on flange locks it in place. Try to center it in whatever you are attaching it to, so it hangs straight. **5 LED IS BEST.** LED bulbs cost a bit more but they stay cool and shine forever. This one's from IKEA, too.

# 14

# make a row of Mason-jar lights

**with Asa Christiana** ● Yet another place to use those IKEA lamp bases is the classic glass Mason jar, the kind made for preserving fruits and vegetables. They hark back to a simpler time and showcase Edison bulbs beautifully—the glowing filaments refracted by the wavy glass. While Mason-jar lights are super-popular right now—online and at your favorite coffee shop—I think the trend is here to stay. They are charming as heck and easy to make.

The practical plus of Mason jars is their tolerance for high heat (part of the canning process for preserving food), so you don't have to worry about them cracking with most bulbs. Just to be safe, though, keep your bulbs to 40 watts max, and drill ventilation holes around the top of the lid (as shown in the project).

As with the lights Mike Warren presented (earlier in this chapter), assembling these lights is the easy part. The trickier part is how to hang them and plug them in. I'll give you one option here, but there are many others.

**RUSTIC CHARM.** A weathered board makes a nice hanger for any number of Mason-jar lights, spaced however you like. Read on for all the how-to.

# DRILL AND ASSEMBLE

Mason jars have a detachable insert in the lid, making it easy to drill the big hole you'll need. After that, assembly is easy.

**1 MARK CENTER.** My combination square comes with a centering attachment. I used it along with an awl to scratch crisscrossing lines at the center of these round parts. **2 PUNCH AND DRILL.** Use an awl to punch small holes in the lid insert, which will guide the hole saw. The saw wants to grab when it breaks through the thin metal, so I clamped it to a board before drilling. The board also protects the table below. **3 ASSEMBLY IS EASY.** Attach the lamp base to the lid insert. Then screw in the Edison bulb and screw the lid onto the jar. **4 ADD A FEW HEAT VENTS.** Use a small drill bit to make holes in the lamp base or jar lid for heat to escape.

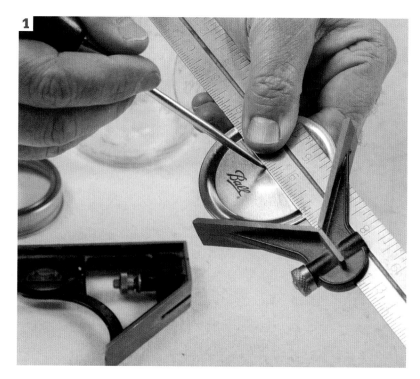

# ONE WAY TO HANG PENDANT LIGHTS

If you don't want to wire each light directly into the ceiling, you can hang them from a board, with one central wire going upward. There are four wires here: three leading down to the lights—with knots on top to hang the lights at the same level—all joined to a single wire up above.

**1 JOIN THE WIRES.** Cut and strip the ends of the wires and wrap them with tape to get them through the holes in the board. Then tie knots in the wires to set the length of the pendants. Now twist all the black wires together and then all the white ones, screwing wire nuts onto the joined ends.

**2 A HANDLE TAKES THE WEIGHT.** The knots will keep the individual lights suspended, but to suspend the entire array, I added a cheap door handle on the top side of the board and knotted the main wire onto that. **3 A FEW STAPLES TAME THE MESS.** I had already cut all the wires as short as possible before joining them, so it took only a few heavy-duty staples to pin them down to the top of the board, mostly out of sight. Now you can hang the main wire off a ceiling hook and run the plug to a wall or ceiling outlet. You might also choose to wire the light right into a ceiling box, or have an electrician do that.

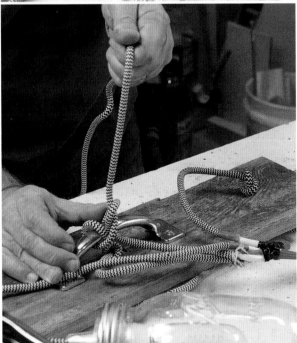

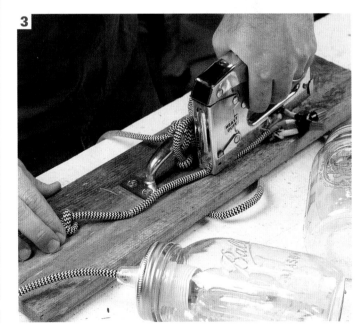

# 6

# two ways to cast the coolest things

MODERN DIY PROJECTS. Working with concrete is pretty simple. Let the projects in this chapter be a starting point for your own designs.

**NO SAMPLER OF** the best DIY techniques would be complete without a chapter on casting. In Chapter 3 you got a taste of the possibilities, with the smooth concrete tops I cast for a pair of 2×4 tables. We pick up the story in this chapter with two more cool projects in concrete from Mike Warren, who presented the IKEA-hacked lights in Chapter 5. Then we invite Scott Grove to blow your mind with cold metal-resin casting, a process that lets you create dozens of metallic objects from the same master pattern.

But let's walk before we run and start with concrete. If you've ever set a fence post in the ground, you know a little about this amazing material. For starters, don't call it "cement." Portland cement is just one of the ingredients in concrete, along with sand and chunks of stone called aggregate. Those premixed ingredients are available at every home center, so all you have to do is add water.

For most purposes, a general concrete mix will work just fine, though there are special formulations that cure faster, work better at cold temperatures, or have smaller bits of rock or sand in them (mortar for masonry is one example). You don't need anything special for the projects in this chapter; just avoid the fast-setting type of concrete that doesn't require mixing.

Speaking of mixing, there are lots of options, including a wheelbarrow, a big tub that sits on the ground, and a rotating barrel you can rent. For the small amount required here, all you need is 5-gal. plastic bucket.

One key to success is getting your batch of concrete mixed and poured before it starts to stiffen, usually 30 minutes or so. After that, you have some additional time to work it. The other key is vibrating the form, to get trapped air bubbles to rise and pop, so you don't see them in the final object. I used a reciprocating saw (sans the blade) to vibrate the form in Chapter 3, but only one of these projects needs to be vibrated, and it's so small that Mike just jiggles and taps the container by hand.

There are endless objects you can cast in concrete, and the two projects in this chapter are just the beginning. If you ever try your hand at building a deck (I hope you do), your concrete skills will help you pour the footings and the landing pads for the stairs. As for me, I plan to pour my own concrete countertops one day and make mixed-media furniture with concrete bases and wood timbers on top.

The beauty of the hands-on life is that one project leads to another as your skills and confidence expand. It's amazing and wonderful how that works.

# balloon candle holders

**with Mike Warren** ○ You met Mike in Chapter 5, and these candle holders are just another example of his brilliance with simple supplies. Who knew you could cast concrete around balloons? These thin globes are a bit fragile, but they're super pretty, and they look just as good if a piece or two breaks off the edges. That said, you should make a few extra, planning for a failure or two.

Mike used Sakrete high-strength concrete mix for this project and the next. Quikrete, a similar product, would work just as well. To avoid breakage with such a thin layer of concrete and to get a smoother surface, he used a

**GOLDEN GLOW.** With a lunar exterior and smooth golden walls, these candle holders add a soft glow to any backyard, porch, or patio.

sieve to remove the bigger pieces of rock before adding water to the mix. You can buy concrete without the aggregate chunks, but it's good to have it in there if you want to use the concrete for other home projects, like the tabletop fireplace on p. 126.

Even the sifted-out gravel gets used in Mike's process, to weigh down paper cups that act as balloon stands (see the step-by-step photos). Once the concrete is mixed and the balloons are ready, you'll be molding your holders by hand and eye, so there are no wrong answers. Do be aware that concrete has an extreme drying effect on skin, and the dust is pretty bad to breathe, so protect yourself.

Mike's other flash of inspiration was painting the inside of his holders metallic gold, to reflect the glow of the tealight candles inside.

**SIMPLE SUPPLIES.** You'll need a 5-gal. bucket, a small sieve, a bag of high-strength concrete, a few paper cups, duct tape, protective gloves, a dust mask, a small trowel, and a bag of large colored balloons. Mike also used a small bottle of metallic acrylic craft paint (not shown) in an antique gold color, plus a few small tealight candles.

# MIX UP THE CONCRETE

**1 SIFT FIRST.** Use a kitchen sieve to filter out the larger rocks and sand, so you get a thin, smooth mix for this project. Save the gravel. **2 THE RIGHT CONSISTENCY.** Add water sparingly and mix well. As always, you want to add just enough water to get the concrete to a peanut butter–like consistency. If it's too wet, just add more concrete mix.

# MOLDING IS FUN

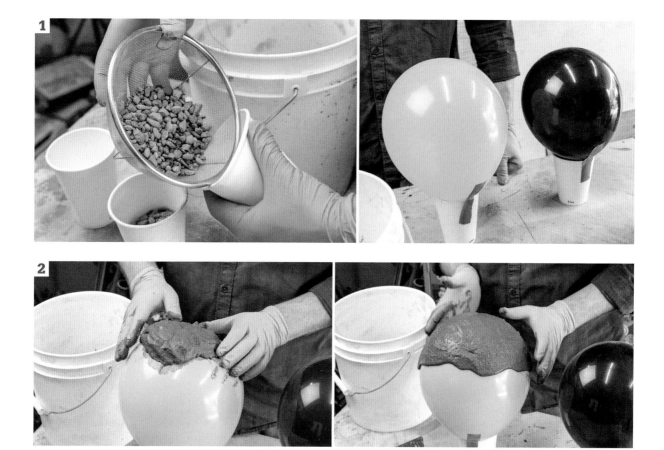

**1 SIMPLE STANDS.** Mike has a slick way to keep the balloons stable as you mold concrete over them. Pour some of the sifted-out rocks into the bottoms of the paper cups to weigh them down a bit. Then blow up the balloons and tape them to the cups.　**2 LET IT GO.** Put a handful of concrete atop the balloon and let it slump downward.　**3 WATCH OUT FOR THIN SPOTS AND HOLES.** The concrete will continue to slump downward until it starts to cure a little, so keep pulling it upward for a few minutes, shaping it however you like, until it begins to stay put. You can also wobble the balloon to spread the concrete. Try to keep the concrete ¼ in. to ⅜ in. thick all over, though a few thin spots aren't bad.

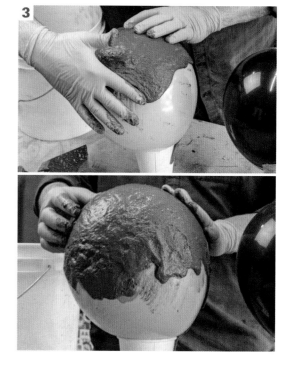

# FINISHING UP

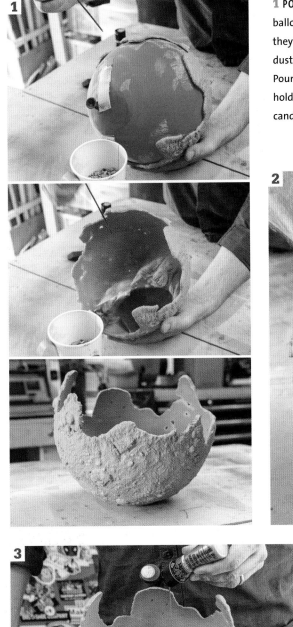

**1** **POP AND MARVEL.** Let the concrete cure overnight and then pop the balloons, leaving behind a lovely object. Handle the holders gently, as they are a bit fragile near the edges. **2** **WIPE THE INSIDE.** Dump out the dust and wipe the inside with a damp paper towel. **3** **MIDAS TOUCH.** Pour antique gold craft paint (or any metallic color you like) inside the holders and spread it with a foam brush. Give it an hour to dry, and the candle holders are ready for their candles.

# 16

# tabletop fireplace

**with Mike Warren** • "There's nothing quite like enjoying a meal by the fire," Mike Warren says. "Now you can have that experience almost anywhere with a portable tabletop fireplace."

This simple concrete tub is propped up with cast-iron feet that give it that industrial feel so many of us love, with a narrow interior that holds two canisters of ethanol-gel chafing fuel (Sterno is a popular brand), surrounded by pebbles or gravel (Mike used concrete aggregate left over from the previous project—no waste!).

As with the candle holders, you don't have to build a form for this project: Mike uses two nested food-storage containers to cast this shallow rectangular tub. Make sure the smaller one is big enough to just hold your Sterno containers and find a larger one big enough to hold the pipe flanges in the

**DINNER BY THE FIRE.** This little portable fireplace will warm up your evenings. It is safe to put on almost any surface and makes anywhere a nicer place to be.

TWO WAYS TO CAST THE COOLEST THINGS

bottom (see p. 128). Try department and dollar stores to find small plastic tubs that will work.

The cast-iron legs are made from plumbing hardware, some pieces galvanized and some not (it doesn't really matter). Mike attaches them by setting the flanges into the bottom of the casting, so the rest of the parts just screw into place afterward.

By the way, thick steel plumbing hardware offers an amazing construction system for makers. It's available at home centers, with all sorts of pipes, joints, and flanges you can combine to create rock-solid furniture and funky lighting, among many other things. The flanges make it easy to attach the pipes to walls, floors, or big slabs of wood, and the cast-iron parts have a vintage industrial look that's both rustic and refined.

**PRO TIP** Sand off any little feet or tabs on the bottom of the inner tub. They'll make it tough to remove that tub from the center after the concrete dries. Also, be sure to leave the aggregate (gravel and rocks) in the concrete mix this time. You need it for full strength.

**SIMPLE SUPPLIES.** To make this project you'll need high-strength concrete mix, two plastic food containers, about $50 worth of $\frac{1}{2}$-in. pipe fittings (flanges, 45° elbows, threaded nipples, and end caps), two clamps, and two Sterno containers. You'll also need a hot-glue gun (not shown).

# DROP IN THE FEET FIRST

**1** **STUFF AND GLUE.** Pack paper towels tightly into the threaded interior of each flange so the concrete doesn't creep in. Then run a bead of hot glue around the top edge.   **2** **FEET GO IN THE CORNERS.** As soon as you squeeze the hot glue onto a flange, drop it immediately into place and leave it there. The glue will keep the feet in place and keep the concrete from getting under the bottom edges.

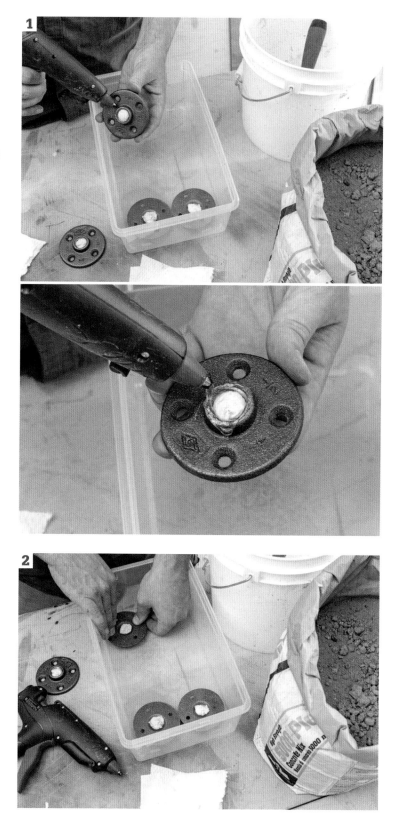

# FILL THE BOTTOM OF THE FORM

**1 FILL IN AROUND THE FEET.** Use a bucket and trowel to mix the concrete to the consistency of peanut butter. And don't sift out the gravel this time. Then shovel some wet concrete into the middle and hold down the flanges as you pack concrete underneath them and into the corners. **2 FILL THE BOTTOM.** Add more concrete and flatten it with the trowel until it's about ½ in. above the flanges. **3 CHECK FOR GAPS.** Take a look at the bottom of the container to be sure the concrete has filled in all around the flanges.

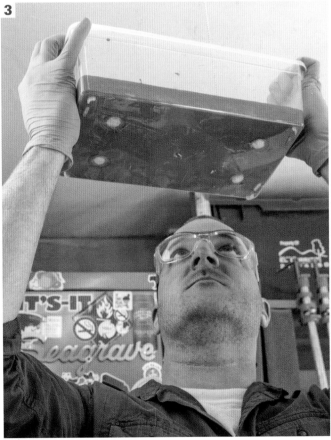

# ADD THE SMALL CONTAINER AND FILL THE SIDES

Mike's smaller tub had open handles in the ends, so he covered those with duct tape.

**1 REINFORCEMENTS.** Press down the small container so it's even, level, and centered, and then clamp the larger tub between wood boards, as shown. These will prevent the heavy concrete from bowing the sides outward.

**2 FILL CAREFULLY.** As you shovel concrete into the sides, hold down the small tub to prevent it from rising. Stop when the trough created in the middle is deep enough to hold the Sterno cans (probably around 2 in.).

**3 RELEASE THE BUBBLES.** While holding down the small tub, tap the large tub on the table to get trapped air bubbles to rise. When they stop rising and popping, you're done. If the small tub has risen a little in the meantime, you can wiggle it back down to the desired level. **4 ADD SOME WEIGHT.** Place a board or a book atop the small container and a weight on top of that, like this bottle of concrete sealer.

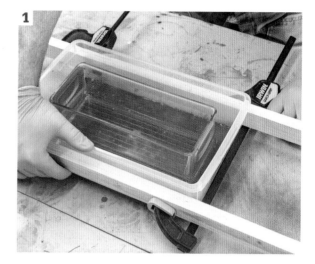

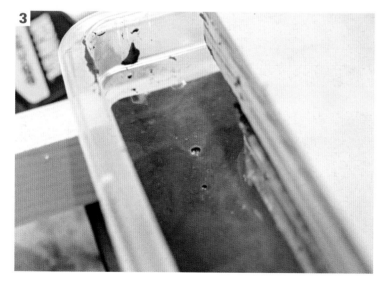

# FINISH UP YOUR FIREPLACE

Let the concrete cure for about four days before removing the forms.

**1 FREE THE CASTING.** Start by pulling it out of the big container, and then squeeze the small container with clamps and work it free with a pair of pliers. Don't be afraid to break it in order to pull it out. **2 POLISHING IS OPTIONAL, BUT VERY NICE.** If you can get your hands on a right-angle grinder, use a 50-grit diamond polishing pad to smooth the top layer and expose the gravel pieces. The dust is nasty, so use a fan to push it out an open window or garage door and wear a mask. **3 PULL THE PLUGS.** Flip over the casting and pull out the paper towels you stuffed in the flanges. Pull off the beads of hot glue, too. **4 SCREW IN THE LEGS.** Threaded nipples connect the flanges to the elbows and the elbows to the end caps. **5 SEAL AND FILL.** Concrete sealer will protect the fireplace from the elements and make the polished edges look really great. Keep wiping it on until the concrete stops drinking it in. Then drop in the Sterno pots and surround them with pebbles. Mike used the aggregate left over from the candle holder project on p. 122.

# 17

# mold one-of-a-kind furniture pulls—and more

**with Scott Grove** • Scott Grove has been crafting fine furniture for a few decades, but he is adept with more than just wood. When he got tired of the furniture hardware available in stores and catalogs, he discovered metal-resin casting. You can use the same molding methods he demonstrates here to cast objects of all kinds, not just furniture pulls.

**BEFORE AND AFTER.** Furniture pulls are just one example of the durable metallic objects you can cast from almost any master. Scott Grove makes his masters (top) from found objects like a pinecone and also crafts them out of wood, in this case adding beads and bark for beautiful effects. He uses the master to make a mold, which is then used to create the final castings (bottom) from a mix of resin and metal powder.

Casting is as easy as baking a cake, and the beauty of this technique is that you can make a master pattern from almost anything, from a found object to a hand-sculpted piece of wood. By adding clay to your master patterns, you can make almost anything work. And you can do it all for less than $5 per casting.

Scott's casting material is a mix of metal powder and urethane resin that creates the look, feel, and durability of real metal without the difficulties of melting and casting it. "I love casting this way," Scott says. "It allows me to make a bronze casting of just about anything, be it a pinecone my wife and I picked up on our honeymoon or my own big toe."

Scott will cover the basic concepts here as he casts a pinecone drawer pull. Once you have the process down, let your imagination run wild.

# WHAT YOU CAN CAST AND WHAT YOU CAN'T

The master is the original object or model that a mold is taken from. This is what your casting will look like exactly—including pores, wrinkles, and even wood grain.

The master doesn't have to be a durable object; it has only to be strong enough for a mold to be taken. So you can use hot-melt glue, clay, or whatever works to create a temporary assemblage. Everyday oil-based clays contain sulfur, which inhibits the curing process of some mold compounds. So Scott uses sulfur-free clay, available from art-supply stores and casting suppliers, and vinyl gloves because latex also can inhibit curing.

Thin areas and minimal contact points are potential areas of failure. For example, if you place a marble on a flat surface with the goal of combining the two, there will be a very small point of contact between them, and the little sphere will break off. But it is easy to use clay to beef up the weak point.

As you plan, you also have to think about how the object will be mounted. The easiest approach is to incorporate areas or elements that will be drilled and tapped for screws and bolts. For this, you need enough meat at the attachment point—for example, at least ³⁄₈ in. of material—to support a #8-32 bolt.

# PLAN FOR THE POUR

Before you can call your master complete, you need to think past making the mold to when you flip the mold over and actually use it. Start by determining where the pouring spout or spouts will be. It should go on the back side of the item, in a hidden or less-visible area. On pulls, Scott often uses the attachment points as spouts.

Not every casting will release all of its air bubbles out of a single spout, so air vents may be needed. These are easy to make, usually by attaching a wooden dowel to the master.

# MAKING A MOLD

While there is a wide variety of molding material to choose from, Scott recommends Smooth-On's Mold Star 16 Fast, which has a low viscosity so it pours and releases bubbles easily. Also, it is very flexible so molds are easy to remove. The "fast" means it offers 6 minutes of working time—perfect for small items like hardware—and takes only 30 minutes to cure.

The first step in making a mold is mounting your master into a "mold box." Typically, Scott mounts it with the pour spout and vent pointing down, using these ports to suspend the master in the middle of the box so it will be completely encompassed by the compound. Leave at least ¹⁄₂ in. of space on all sides and on top. This mold box can be simple, like a plastic cup or a plywood or melamine box.

If you make a box, seal the inside corners with clay, caulk, or hot-melt glue so the compound won't leak out. Also, fasten the master to the bottom of the box with hot-melt glue so it won't move or float.

To avoid mixing up too much mold compound and wasting it, do some simple math to calculate the volume of the container. You can also pour water in and pour it out to measure.

## THE CASTING PROCESS

For small parts like the ones seen here, Scott uses a two-part urethane resin called Smooth-Cast Onyx Slow, also made by Smooth-On. It's a one-to-one mix, which is one reason he loves it. It allows 5 minutes of working time and cures hard in 90 minutes. Scott uses the black color (onyx) with darker metal powders, such as bronze, copper, and brass, and a white variety with lighter metal powders such as aluminum and nickel-silver.

Before you make your first metal-resin casting, always make a sample with the urethane resin only, to test the quality of the mold and clean out any residue. At the same time, check that the seams align and the vents are working. If you discover any trapped air, you can always drill an extra vent through the mold, so don't worry.

## SIMPLE SUPPLIES

There are a host of supplies for casting, but the materials shown below are among the easiest to use for small pieces like furniture pulls. All are available from Smooth-On.

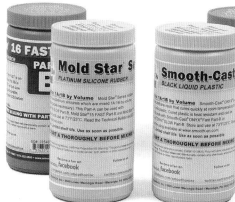

**SILICONE MOLD MATERIAL.**
Mold Star 16 Fast, trial unit (2 lb.).

**METAL POWDER.**
Bronze powder (brass, copper, aluminum, and nickel-silver also available), 1-lb. container.

**URETHANE CASTING MATERIAL.**
Smooth-Cast Onyx Slow, trial size (2.2 lb.). This color works well with darker metal powders. Use the white variety for lighter ones like aluminum and nickel-silver.

# MAKE A MASTER

A found object like this pinecone makes a beautiful custom pull, but only after a few extra steps are taken.

**1 FILL DEEP CREVICES.** This will make the mold easier to remove. Use sulfur-free modeling clay and wipe off the excess with petroleum jelly. **2 ADD A MOUNTING POST.** Again, clay works well and can be textured with modeling tools. This mounting post will double as the pour spot for the casting process. **3 ADD A VENT IF NEEDED.** The stem of the pinecone will point upward during the casting process, trapping an air bubble. A thin dowel, supported by more clay and attached with hot-melt glue, provides an air vent.

# THEN USE IT TO MAKE A MOLD

A yogurt container works great for a small 3-D object, while melamine (particleboard) boxes can be made for flatter objects. Attach the master to the bottom with hot-melt glue.

**1 MIX AND POUR.** Mix the two-part mold material thoroughly and pour it into one spot on the bottom of the container, never on the object itself. Tap the sides to release any bubbles. A line in the cup marks the best place to cut the mold open later. **2 STRATEGIC CUTS.** Scott made cuts at both ends of the pinecone with a long razor knife, feeling for the vent dowel at one end and the surface of the pinecone at the other, and cutting down only as far as necessary to extract the object.

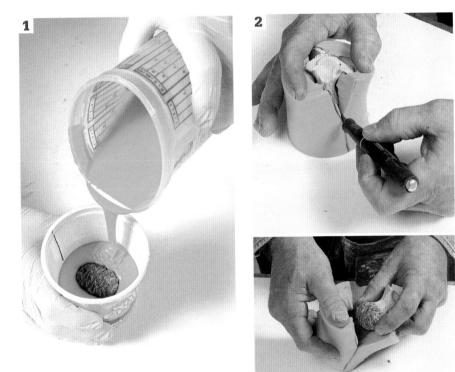

# CASTING A PULL

A rubber band will reclose round molds, while rectangular ones can be lightly clamped. Do a first casting without metal powder to reveal any problems and extract debris from the mold. Add metal powder when you are ready to cast for real.

**1 DUST AND SHAKE.** Dusting the mold with metal powder ensures that the metal color will be even on the outside of the casting. Cover the spout and vents and shake to coat all surfaces. Then shake out the excess powder. **2 MIX AND POUR.** Mix up the two-part urethane and then mix in the metal powder. Don't go thicker than the consistency of honey. Pour the mixture in slowly and steadily.

# Scott Grove

A third-generation artist, Scott Grove designs and creates in many modes: architectural reproductions, photography, murals, play spaces, interiors, film, and more. As a professional furnituremaker and sculptor, he's known for unconventional methods and materials, including found objects, carved textures, veneers, and unusual finishes. His work is a part of the permanent collection in the Hunter Museum of American Art in Chattanooga, Tenn., and the Memorial Art Gallery in Rochester, N.Y., and has received many awards. He also holds workshops nationally on design, specialty finishes, veneering, mold making, and fiberglass construction. He maintains a workshop in downtown Rochester, where he produces commission work and speculative art as well as limited-edition pieces. Check out scottgrove.com to see a few decades of his amazing work.

TWO WAYS TO CAST THE COOLEST THINGS

# A FEW FINISHING TOUCHES

**1 EASY OUT.** The pliable silicone mold material makes it easy to remove castings. **2 TRIM THE CASTING.** The urethane resin can be worked like wood. Saw off the vent, trim the paper-thin flashing at the seams, saw off some of the base, and then flatten it on sandpaper. **3 DRILL AND TAP.** The casting can be drilled and tapped easily for common bolt sizes. A tap is a hand-fed thread cutter. **4 BURNISH AND ADD DEPTH.** Burnish with steel wool to reveal the metal and then wipe dark shoe polish or black wax into the cracks and crevices to add depth and detail.

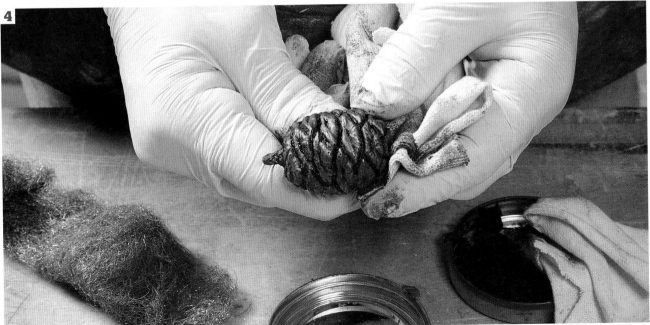

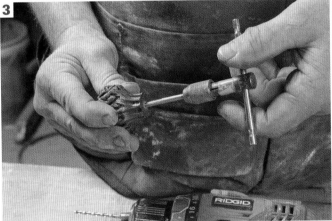

# 7

# printmaking: unlock your inner artist

**TRY SCREEN PRINTING.**
The photo-emulsion process creates screens with crisp detail, which deliver prints of the same quality.

**BEFORE I WROTE** this book I knew next to nothing about the rich world of printmaking. I was aware that my musician friends were screen-printing their own "merch," and I've always admired the elemental contrast and hand-carved quality of woodblock prints, but I had only the vaguest idea how either process really worked. So I was tough on potential printmakers for this book. "How doable is this for a beginner?" I asked. "Totally," the two artists answered. "Aren't the tools expensive?" "Not at all."

As they went through the basic steps for each process and sent me pics of sample projects, I really started smiling. The printmaking technology in this chapter ranges from ancient to brand new, but the steps are straightforward, the results are amazing, and both projects are unmistakably handcrafted.

The other hurdle was whether these items are actually "things you use every day," as promised on the cover. T-shirts definitely are, for all but the most dapper among us.

As for Japanese woodblock prints, if this book is about surrounding yourself with handmade beauty, how can we ignore the walls? Also, art serves a very practical purpose: It inspires.

Like so many maker projects, some printmaking methods are hard to categorize cleanly. The wood block requires a fair amount of carving (moderately easy and majorly fun), which could have landed it in the wood chapter. Also, while Chris Gardner covers a tried-and-true screen-printing technique here, Chamisa Kellogg offers a cool high-tech variation in Chapter 8.

## YOU DON'T HAVE TO DRAW TO MAKE GREAT PRINTS

I know how to build things, but I hesitate to call myself an artist, mostly because I don't draw very well. If you can draw beautiful things freehand, you'll be able to put that skill to good use in this chapter, turning a beautiful picture into piles of T-shirts, tote bags, prints, and posters of all kinds. But if you can't, there are great workarounds. Either way, you'll be using your own eye to turn the design into something personal and unique.

For the screen-printed motif, I combined royalty-free clip art with Japanese characters to create a design for nature lovers worldwide, which Chris Gardner tweaked in Adobe Illustrator to suit his own sensibility. For the woodblock prints, Timothy Hamilton decided against a freehand drawing (he is more than capable) and went with a compelling photo and a simple process for transferring its essential lines to plywood. In both cases, there was plenty of room left for artistic interpretation.

But this book is more about practical techniques than the specific designs. I can't wait to see what you cook up on your own.

# 18 screen-print your own T-shirts

**with Chris Gardner** • As the content creator for two major DIY websites—Curbly (curbly.com) and ManMade (manmadediy.com)—Chris Gardner spends most of his time designing projects and explaining the steps to makers of all skill levels. So when he told me he had done a lot of screen printing, I knew he was just the guy to teach the basics in this book.

There are lots of ways to make screens, like the one in the next chapter, but this is the technique most pros use, capable of transferring almost any design with perfect detail, thanks to a light-sensitive photo emulsion. That might sound scary, but it is super easy to do and really fun.

**THE MAKER IN HIS NATURAL HABITAT.** Avid hikers both, Chris Gardner (pictured here) and I designed our shirt around the Japanese concept of "forest bathing." The characters form the words *shinrin-yoku*, the simple medicine of being in the forest.

**EVERYTHING YOU NEED.**

The excellent All-In-One Fabric Screen Printing Kit from Speedball has almost everything you need for photo-emulsion screen printing, including the screen, transparency film, and exposure lamp; the components for creating the emulsion and washing it off; and a nice set of fabric inks. You'll need to add a yellow bug light (which will let you see in a dark room but won't expose the emulsion), some upholstery foam, and your shirts of choice.

No matter how you make the screens, screen printing lets you crank out endless shirts, posters, and other prints for friends and family. Armed with the photo-emulsion technique, you might even turn pro, selling your brilliant designs online and at local craft shows.

You can buy screen-printing supplies separately, but you'll save time and money with a kit like the one Chris used here. Speedball is the leader in the field, and their Advanced All-in-One Fabric Screen Printing Kit is less than $100 from art-supply stores like Dick Blick Art Materials (dickblick.com). Designed for printing on fabric, it comes with everything you need, including a 10-in. by 14-in. screen, a squeegee, the emulsion mixture, the lamp for exposing the screen, and even a starter set of quality fabric inks—everything but the T-shirts.

## WHY THE PHOTO-EMULSION METHOD RULES

One of the cool things about making screens with the light-sensitive emulsion is that they can be washed out afterward and remade with new patterns on them. Other than a dark closet or small room with no windows, all you need to print a pile of shirts is a table, a sink, and a desktop printer.

Like I said up front, you don't need to be an artist to make amazing prints. With the photo-emulsion process, if you can create a design on your computer— using clip art, fonts, and so on—and you own a working printer, you can make a perfect screen. Here's why.

After you have a design you like, you print it in black on transparency film. Then, working in a dark room with a yellow bug bulb for light, you squeegee the emulsion onto the screen and place the transparency on top. Now when you hang the exposure lamp over the screen, the light hardens the emulsion only where it hits, leaving the shielded areas soft. Back in the light again, you head to the kitchen sink, where you wash out the soft emulsion that wasn't exposed. Presto, you have a precise opening in the screen for the ink to pass through.

It takes a little practice to dial in the amount of ink to apply, but you can make prints on paper before committing to your shirts. Also, it's very easy to position the cardboard a little off-center when placing it inside the shirt. At that point, you'll probably place the screen and the design off-center, too. So be careful when folding the shirt around the cardboard.

One last note: Fabric inks will last much longer if you heat-set them after they fully dry. It's easy to do with a household iron. Check the instructions that come with your kit or visit Speedball's website at speedballart.com for helpful how-tos.

Welcome to the not-so-secret world of screen printing. Tell your friends how cool and easy it is, and Chris's nefarious plan will be complete.

# GET READY

There is some prep work to do before you head into a darkened room and start mixing up the light-sensitive emulsion.

**1 REFINE YOUR DESIGN.** You can create a pattern in any word-processing or graphics program. Chris used Adobe Illustrator, importing the royalty-free art and Japanese characters we found online, then refining their size and spacing. Be sure to fill in any outlines with solid black.   **2 PRINT A TRANSPARENCY.** The kit includes plastic transparency film for ink-jet printers. If you have a laser printer or copier, you'll need a different type of film. Be sure to print in black only.   **3 CUT SOME FOAM.** You can skip this step, but Chris recommends packing upholstery foam into the screen frame to improve the exposure process. Cut it about ½ in. larger than the interior of the frame in both directions.   **4 SEAL THE EDGES.** You don't want water, ink, or the emulsion to get between the screen and the wood frame, so seal the inside edges with blue painter's tape.

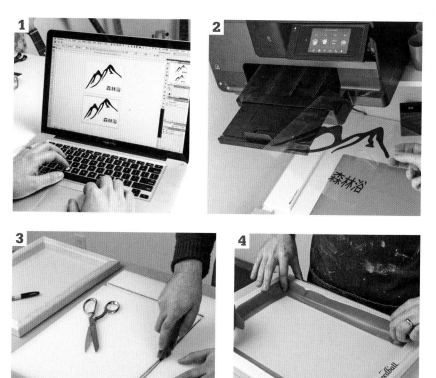

# INTO THE YELLOW ROOM

Find a closet or small room that can be sealed off from all but the tiniest light leaks. Turn off the lights in the adjoining room too. Then insert a yellow bug bulb into a lamp or overhead light. It will provide plenty of visibility without exposing the emulsion.

**1 MAGIC POTION.** To activate the emulsion liquid, mix in the small bottle of light sensitizer.   **2 COAT THE SCREEN.** Pour out a bead of the emulsion and spread it across one side of the screen. Do the same thing on the other side, but spread it perpendicular to the first pass.   **3 WAIT A WHILE.** Lean the screen upright and leave it in the dark at least 4 hours. The emulsion will be dry to the touch but still soft. If you need to leave it longer than 4 hours, you can wrap it in a sealed box or thick, black trash bag to keep it in this ready state for up to 2 weeks.

# EXPOSE THE SCREEN

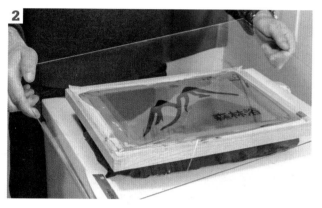

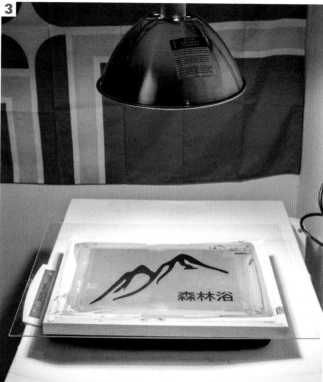

The key is pressing the transparency evenly against the emulsion, so light comes through only where you want it to, with no leakage around the edges of your design.

**1 PACK THE BACK.** Use the upholstery foam and some black fabric (a T-shirt works) to fill the back of the frame with a smooth, black surface. This will press the front of the screen flat against the transparency, ensuring minimal light leakage and a crisp transfer. **2 STACK THE FRONT.** Lay down the transparency (it should be backward here—we fixed it shortly afterward), spacing it evenly on the screen, and place a layer of glass on top to hold it down. **3 LET THERE BE LIGHT.** Hang the exposure lamp directly over the screen at the recommended height and start the timer. The Speedball emulsion takes 8 minutes to harden. Any longer than that, and it could harden so much it will be difficult to remove later, making it hard to reuse the screen. **4 PRESTO.** Now you can head out into the light, find a sink, and wash out the unhardened areas of the screen. Use your fingers to rub the soft emulsion off both sides. What's left are the exposed, hardened areas that weren't covered by the black image on the transparency.

# Chris Gardner

Chris Gardner is the brain (and hands) behind two popular DIY websites, curbly.com and manmadediy.com. The first focuses on home decor, and the other presents a wide variety of projects and lifestyle tips for hands-on guys like him. But both land squarely in the heart of the handcrafted movement.

With science teachers for parents, it was inevitable that Chris would grow up with chemistry sets, microscopes, slides, and kits for growing crystals, and maybe also inevitable that he would put his own twist on the projects. "I was always more interested in the tools and the materials and the process than creating the thing on the cover of the box," he says. "It didn't always turn out good, but I didn't care."

Before long, Chris started making short films with his friends, with handmade props and special effects. When he joined a punk band, he loved the DIY aspect of the whole scene—basement shows, hand-printed posters, and record labels started in garages. The first T-shirt he screen-printed was for the band.

Chris's DIY spirit went dormant in college but came back to life when he fixed up his first apartment. Like lots of makers in the 2000s, he was inspired by *ReadyMade* magazine, learning all sorts of inexpensive ways he could improve his surroundings. "I was used

to songwriting and making little movies, which was so abstract," he says. "Making stuff for my house and everyday life had an immediate payoff. I got to spend time learning new tools and techniques, and get to use them in a real-world context."

Soon after, Chris found curbly.com. He became a regular contributor and was hired as the site's editor-in-chief in 2010. The site he created later, ManMade, was born out of his experience as "a man in this 'indie craft' world," he says. "I kept waiting for someone to translate the techniques to a masculine point of view (men don't make clothes with bust-waist-hips measurements). Eventually, I realized that person should probably be me."

# TIPS FOR SUCCESSFUL PRINTING

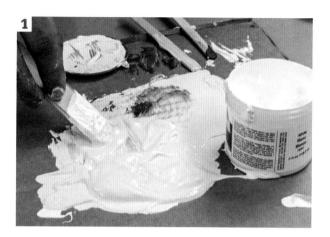

Don't wait long between prints or the ink left in the screen will begin to dry and clog the mesh. Iron the shirts and place a piece of cardboard inside one of them, to have it ready for printing. Then do a trial run on paper to dial in your technique before screen-printing a shirt.

**1 MIX UP YOUR INK.** To give the white ink a vintage look, Chris mixed in red, yellow, and blue to add a sepia tone.

**2 DIAL IN YOUR TECHNIQUE.** Make a print on paper first. Put down plenty of ink so one firm swipe across the screen does the job. If you come back in the other direction, you may force ink under the edges of the pattern. When your paper prints look good, start printing shirts.    **3 PRINT T-SHIRTS!** With the cardboard centered below the front of the shirt, you can center the screen over the cardboard to align your print. Lay down a thick bead of ink and make a firm swipe with the squeegee. Then raise the screen to see your handiwork. Remove the cardboard and lay out the T-shirt carefully to dry. After it dries for a day, you should heat-set the ink with an iron. Check the instructions that come with your kit.

# 19

# learn Japanese woodblock printing

**with Timothy Hamilton** • Woodblock prints have a hand-carved look that is impossible to reproduce any other way. There are a few good ways to approach it, so I worked hard to find the best one for this book. That led me to Timothy Hamilton, who went to school for printmaking and teaches the Japanese woodblock method at a big makerspace. This traditional Japanese process is done completely by hand, with simple tools, at low cost; and it makes unmatched prints of any size. It takes a little practice to master the subtleties, but all that requires is some extra ink and paper.

The first thing you'll learn with this project is how to transfer a picture to wood and carve a block. You can then use that block any way you like. If it's small you can use it as a stamp, inking it on a pad and pressing it down on nice paper products to make cards or whatever.

**GOOD STARTING POINT.**
Timothy started with a photo of the St. Johns Bridge in Portland, playing with the color in Photoshop and sizing it to fit a standard paper roll.

With this technique, you can pause to lay down subtle color or just skip straight to the hard lines. Note the carved swirls that bring the clouds to life. A simple glass frame works well with these handmade prints.

But if it's a full-size image, like the 8½-in. by 11-in. print Timothy made here, the stamp technique won't work. It's too hard to get even pressure and a consistent print with a big wood stamp, unless you use an expensive rolling press.

So for larger prints, printmakers flip the elements. The block goes down first, face up. Then it gets inked and the paper goes on top, where it is rubbed with some sort of tool to be sure it touches the block in all areas. Lift the paper and the print is done. The wood block never moves, and you can manipulate the ink and paper with amazing control.

## JAPANESE METHOD HAS MANY ADVANTAGES

There are variations on this basic approach, and Timothy used them all before settling on the Japanese technique. The inking stage requires some practice, but the results are subtle, rich, and astounding. Because the ink is applied to the woodblock in dots and dabs and adjusted with a brush—as opposed to rolled on in one swoop—you can create textures and gradients not possible with other methods—even multiple colors at once. In addition, the Japanese technique offers more

precision in how the paper (and print) is positioned and how the top side is rubbed to transfer the print.

With the Japanese technique, the edges of the paper are registered in two indentations you carve into the block, called *kento* marks, which make it easy to drop the paper in the same spot every time.

To convey the other advantages and all the basic techniques, Timothy chose a picture with hard lines and soft color, which he tackles in two steps, using the "suicide" printing technique. Instead of carving two separate blocks, one for the soft color stage (called *bokashi*) and one for the hard lines, he carved only some of the lines at first, leaving big flat areas for the color. After making a bunch of prints that way, he cut the rest of the lines in the block, relieved all the other areas, and printed the hard lines and shapes on top of the soft color.

With the reductive suicide technique, you've only got one shot at applying the bokashi color, so you need

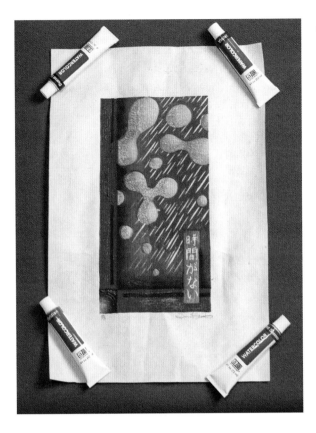

to make plenty of prints at that stage—as many as you are likely to want, plus a few extra for practice and mistakes. The advantages, however, are easier registration and a clear view of where the soft color should go in relation to the hard lines.

## LEARN BASIC WOODCARVING

Rhythmic, methodical, and absorbing, carving is downright addictive. With just a few basic tools in hand and a few basic techniques under your belt, you can fire up your Bluetooth speaker and get lost in the process. Timothy carved the detailed block shown in the following pages in less than an hour, using a simple set of carving gouges. A beginner can do it in two at the most.

Because the carving is shallow relief work in a thin plywood panel, you can use small, inexpensive

**ENDLESS POSSIBILITIES.** Timothy's work suggests the unlimited potential of this versatile technique.

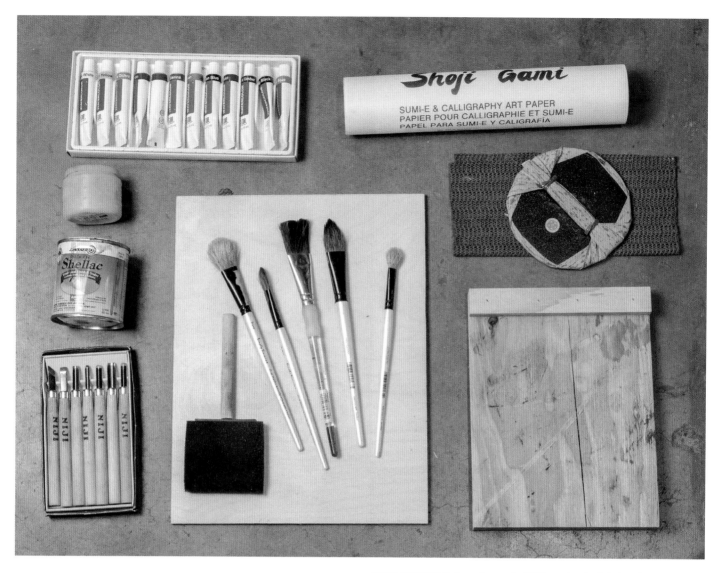

gouges and move quickly. One key is understanding wood grain. Depending on how the wood is cut out of the log, the grain can run through the board in various ways. Cut in the right direction and it will feel like petting a dog; carve against the grain and the gouge wants to plunge and tear the wood. That means you need to move the board around a lot as you work, trying cuts from different directions. You'll get a feel for the grain in your specific workpiece as you go.

Once you learn to carve a big woodblock like this one, you might try carving smaller ones to use as stamps or move on to some other sort of carving, like spoons or furniture parts. There's something satisfying about hand-tool woodworking that has captivated generations of artisans, including the current one.

**SIMPLE SUPPLIES.** A 12-piece set of Niji carving tools is just $10 to $15, and the amber shellac, rice paste (nori), watercolor paint set (in tubes), wove art paper (sold for sumi-e ink and calligraphy), disk baren (round pressure pad), flat art brushes, foam brush, thin sanded plywood, and other supplies are inexpensive, too. At the bottom right is a simple shopmade bench hook, and the material under the disk baren is rubber shelf liner.

Here are a few final tips: It's important to control the carving tools with two hands, one to push the gouge and another to guide it. So you need some way to anchor the wood block and leave your hands free. Two good ways are shown in this project. Also, these prints are watercolor, so they are best protected behind glass.

# PREP YOUR BLOCK

The goal here is to darken the wood a bit, so as you carve, the block will look like the print: dark where it will be dark and white where it will be white.

**1 LOOK FOR THIN PLIES.** Use ¼-in.-thick, sanded plywood with multiple plies to make your wood block. The smooth plywood acts a lot like the solid-wood edge grain used traditionally, but the internal glue lines help it soak up less ink and resist warping. They also help you gauge depth as you carve. **2 STAIN THE SURFACE.** Use a thin wash of red watercolor to stain the surface of the plywood. Soak up the excess moisture with a paper towel and let the wood dry for at least 5 minutes. **3 ADD SOME SHELLAC.** Amber-colored shellac adds more color and seals the wood so not as much ink soaks in. Wipe on a quick coat, let it dry for a few hours, and then smooth off the wood whiskers with 320-grit sandpaper. **4 SHELF LINER HOLDS IT IN PLACE.** Rubberized shelf liner material is one way to keep the board from moving while you carve.

# TRANSFER THE DESIGN

There are lots of ways to transfer the essential lines of a design to the wood, like using carbon paper, but the following method is the simplest.

**1 LOCATE THE PAPER.** Cut a piece to final size, square it up on the block, and make a few pencil marks at the bottom corners.   **2 TRACING TRICK.** Use a No. 2 pencil to trace over all the lines you want to transfer. This will make visible dents on the back side. Now flip the paper, place it on the wood block, and retrace those same indented lines. This will transfer the pencil marks from the paper to the wood.   **3 DARKEN THE LINES.** Trace over the fine lines and impressions on the wood to make clear marks for carving. Don't hesitate to draw some lines freehand.   **4 DRAW A BORDER, TOO.** Guide your pencil with a ruler for this step.

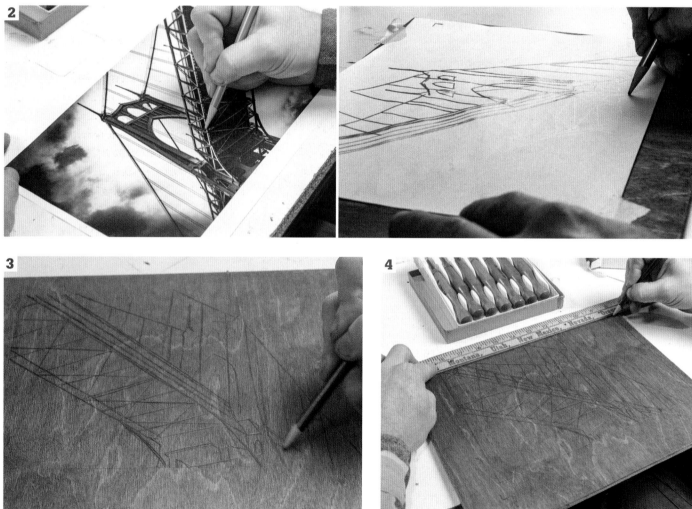

# CARVE REGISTRATION MARKS

Kento marks are deep indentations that locate the bottom corner of the paper on the left side and just the bottom edge on the right. Try to carve to the depth of two sheets of paper, or down to the first glue line in the plywood.

**1 CHECK YOUR PAPER.** Timothy sized his design to fit the paper roll, then laid the roll on the block to position the registration marks. **2 LEFT-HAND MARK TURNS THE CORNER.** Start by making deep cuts with the straight carving knife, with its bevel facing inward. Then use the shallow gouge to carve inside the vertical line and inside the horizontal one at the bottom. **3 GO DEEPER AND WIDER.** Deepen the indentation and relieve the areas outside the ends too, so it's easy to insert the corner of the paper in the pocket. **4 RIGHT-HAND MARK IS EASIER.** The indentation on the right side is just a flat stop for the bottom edge of the paper. Use the same process: straight knife then shallow gouge.

# FIRST PRINTING REQUIRES MINIMAL CARVING

To print the soft blue halo, Timothy carved away any details in the blue areas that he wanted to remain white in the final print.

**1 RELIEVE THE BORDER.** Start by knifing along the border lines, with the bevel of the knife facing outward this time, and then use a wide gouge to relieve everything outside that line down to the first glue line in the plywood. Note the simple bench hook that holds the block well when you are carving squarely across it.   **2 CARVE THE HIGHLIGHTS.** Timothy used a V-gouge to create the highlights along the steel bridge parts and a small curved gouge to make the little swirls in the clouds. He also pulled up any splinters that would have kept the paper from lying flat on the inked areas.   **3 PRACTICE THE PAPER DROP.** Before inking the block, practice setting the paper in the registration marks (left side first then right), anchoring it there with your thumbs and letting it drop.

# PRINT 1: BRUSH UP ON YOUR BOKASHI

Bokashi is the technique of applying paint selectively to flat areas of the wood block and manipulating it with a brush. With the suicide carving technique, you have only one crack at this print run, so make enough copies to perfect your technique and have all the prints you might want later.

**1 WATER, INK, BRUSH.** The bokashi technique is all about keeping the ink wet, so start by brushing on some water. Then lay down a few strategic dots of ink and spread and swirl it with the brush. The goal is a gradient, with thinner color at the edges. **2 NOT TOO MUCH WATER.** After applying water or rinsing out the brush, always squeeze it out. And feel free to dab the inked block with a tissue to soak up any water puddles. **3 NOW PRINT FOR REAL.** Anchor the paper in the registration marks and drop it as before. **4 COVER AND RUB.** Lay down a double sheet of newsprint, which will protect the wove paper and help keep it from moving. Then rub the cloud areas with the disk baren to transfer ink to paper. Start by pressing the baren straight down to anchor the paper on some of the ink, and then move it around in small circles. **5 CHECK YOUR WORK.** Pull up the paper from one edge. If you aren't happy with the results, try adding more ink or water next time and feel free to do more carving if necessary. Then make as many prints as you need, washing off the block each time.

# CARVE THE REST OF THE PATTERN

The hard lines are next, so relieve every part of the panel that you don't want to transfer ink to the paper.

**1 OUTLINE THE RELIEF AREAS.** Start with a V-gouge and cut lines around the outside of every area you plan to relieve, leaving the lines you want to print. **2 CARVE BETWEEN THE LINES.** Use curved gouges to carve out the relief areas, working down to the first dark glue line in the plywood, maybe farther. The bigger the relief area, the deeper you need to carve to keep the paper from touching down. **3 MISTAKES ARE EASY TO FIX.** Occasionally, you'll push too hard near an edge and break off an area you wanted to keep. Just put some yellow glue on the back of the chip, press it into place, and leave that area alone for a couple of hours. **4 TAKE YOUR TIME.** There is a lot to carve in a block like this one, with big relief areas and lots of fine lines, but the work is steady and satisfying.

# Timothy Hamilton

**M**ilitary service ran in the family for Timothy Hamilton, and he saw it as a practical way to pay for college without running up debt. He chose the Army because that branch let him pick his job. His test scores qualified him to become an intelligence officer, so he signed up while still in high school, opting for delayed entry. It was February 2001. A few months before basic training, two planes flew into the World Trade Center, and Timothy's military career took a turn.

He did two tours in Iraq over four years, analyzing troop positions, tracking enemy activity, and planning missions. He enjoyed working in a compact, four-person unit, and the trust commanders put in them. And he was able to remain mostly out of danger, though he came close to being ambushed once. What he didn't like was the extreme chaos and constant lack of clarity. "You're just doing the best you can until you can go home," he says.

Back in Oregon, Timothy did two more years in the National Guard, where he was almost "stop-lossed" and sent back to Iraq before a kind company commander put him in a support detachment that couldn't be deployed.

He attended the University of Oregon on the GI Bill, graduating with a BFA in sculpture, and followed it up with a master's in visual studies at Minneapolis College of Art and Design. He studied printmaking in both colleges and taught the subject at MCAD.

Timothy returned to Oregon to outfit a camper van and live on his parents' property, landing a contract job making trophies for a film festival in the Twin Cities. Needing more serious tools and machines, he discovered ADX, Portland's big makerspace. He became a shop steward, joined ADX's professional fabrication team, and now serves as education director while filling out his professional art portfolio. His goal is a permanent college teaching job, and he's well on his way.

# PRINT 2: THE HARD LINES

Practice makes perfect at this stage also, but you don't need to wash the block between your attempts. The key to success is applying an even film of water, paste, and ink, making sure the whole block is wet before you lay down the paper.

**1 THICKENER FIRST.** After wetting the block with water, apply a paint thickener. Rice paste (nori) is the traditional option, but any watercolor thickener will work. Apply it strategically so you can spread it around the printed areas. **2 THEN INK.** Apply dots strategically, a little extra at first when the wood is clean and bare. Then spread the ink and paste evenly with a brush. **3 AN EVEN COAT EVERYWHERE.** Apply ink and paste to the hard lines too, using only what's left on the brush or applying more from the paste pot and ink tube. Look at the block in low-angle light to find blobs of paint or paste and areas that are too dry.

**4 PRINT LIKE BEFORE.** Anchor the paper in the kento marks, let it drop, cover it with newsprint, and rub with the disk baren. Try to bridge the relief areas without dipping into them. Before lifting the paper, check the back side for even absorption and locate areas that might need more rubbing. **5 PRACTICE ON PLAIN PAPER FIRST, WITHOUT BOKASHI COLOR.** Feel free to carve the relief areas deeper if they are touching the paper. When you get a clean, dark transfer like the one shown, you are ready to use the prints with soft color on them. **6 PRINTING GETS EASIER AS YOU GO.** You'll be leaving the excess ink and paste on the wood block, so you won't have to apply as much for later prints. It's a great feeling when you master your technique and start making one nice print after another.

# level up with digital tools

**LASERS AND LEDS.**
This laser-cut sign is just the beginning of what you can build with digital tools and supplies.

**THE MAKER MOVEMENT** emerged from hacker culture, which shadowed the computer revolution from its earliest days, proving that the urge to make something personal cannot be defeated.

While the microchip was driving mass-production and mass-marketing to new levels and delivering mesmerizing new forms of passive entertainment, it was also powering new tools for making things independently, one at time, like CAD software, 3-D printers, laser cutters, vinyl cutters, and open-source microprocessors.

These high-tech tools for making real things drew the first makers away from their screens and back to the bench, helping launch a resurgence in handcrafts of all sorts, powered by the Web. We also have digital tools to thank for the rise of the makerspace, which answered the demand for access to this exciting new equipment.

Whether you're attracted to the hands-on life by old technology or new, you can't afford to ignore digital tools. The earliest artisans embraced every new technology they could get their hands on, and I don't know why anyone would avoid doing the same today.

## THIS CHAPTER IS JUST A TASTE

The makers in this chapter use design software and digital cutters to make things that would be extremely difficult otherwise, and take advantage of inexpensive electronics that weren't available a generation ago.

The first project is Rob Leifheit's illuminated signs, with laser-cut masks and LED lights. The next two projects demonstrate the power of the vinyl cutter. Here, Chamisa Kellogg uses it to create an entire branding suite, with a self-adhesive vinyl sign for a wall or window and the same design used to create a screen for printing branded items with the same logo. The same way Wix and Squarespace make it easy to create your online storefront, the vinyl cutter makes it easy to create a branded business, even if it's just for fun.

These digital tools are just a taste of what's out there. Laser cutters and 3-D printers are getting less expensive by the minute, and small vinyl cutters cost as little as $200. And if you want to try bigger, more-powerful models of all of the above, you'll find them at your local makerspace, college, or other community workshop.

I left Arduino out of the mix, but you should definitely check it out on your own. It's just one of the open-source systems for building and programming cheap DIY circuit boards, to control all sorts of motors, LEDs, and other mechanical devices. Today's makers combine hand-assembled, self-programmed microcontrollers with 3-D printed parts for DIY drones, games, robotics, and countless other digital devices. Microcontrollers are what drive all of your household appliances, so they can be made to do almost anything. If electronic gizmos give you goosebumps, check out *Make:* magazine and Instructables (instructables.com) for hundreds of project ideas.

# 20 programmable LED signs

### with Rob Leifheit ● Rob Leifheit creates electronic signs by cutting custom masks with a 3-D printer or laser cutter and lighting them up with programmable LEDs. The sign he built for this book keeps everything as simple as possible without compromising any of the magic.

Instead of a DIY circuit board driving the diodes, he went with his other favorite option, a $10 LED controller, which requires no programming at all. It's just one more cool new digital gizmo available online for next to nothing. Solder the controller to a strip of addressable LEDs, and the little wireless remote will make your sign do 100 different dances.

To cut the mask, Rob rented an hour at a digital-fabrication space in Los Angeles to get access to their big laser cutter. He has a smaller model in his home shop, but the industrial version at the Build Shop let him

**TWO SIGNS IN ONE.** Rob interpreted one of my favorite mottos in two ways, one with walnut plywood, simple letters, and a repeating pattern engraved on the front (left); the other on birch plywood with a graphic element in the middle (right).

**MAKE IT YOUR OWN.** The LED controller comes with a little remote that can make the lights change in dozens of ways.

**ELECTRONIC PARTS**

- 5-volt to 12-volt controller for ws2811 and ws2812b RGB LED strips, $10
- Small roll of addressable LED strip lights, 30 per meter, with self-adhesive back, $10
- 5-volt DC wall power adapter, $8
- 3-ft. USB to type-M-barrel DC power cable, $18
- Small roll of three-strand, 20 AWG wire for LEDs, $8

cut through the ¼-in.-thick plywood we used for our masks and engrave a repeating pattern on the surface.

Rob created two different masks for this project and had time to cut them both in one $20 session. (He didn't need guidance, but professional assistance is just $10 per hour more at the Build Shop in LA.)

## LASER CUTTER OR NOT, YOU CAN STILL MAKE A SIGN

If you don't have access to a laser cutter, any opaque material will work for the mask, including paper and vinyl, and you can cut out the design with a vinyl cutter, X-Acto knife, scissors, scrollsaw, or blow torch. Either way, the LEDs will do their thing.

Instead of building the sign housing by hand, Rob headed to that same purveyor of Swedish meatballs mentioned earlier in this book, and found a deep 9-in. by 9-in. Ribba picture frame that works perfectly. To

diffuse the light, he pulled the clear acrylic out of the front of the frame and replaced it with milky-white plastic. That diffuser, together with the frame's 1¾-in. depth, lets the colors shine through without revealing the individual diodes.

You'll also need roughly $55 worth of electronic components, but the wire and LEDs come in rolls, so you'll have lots left over for other projects. To combine the electronics, you'll need some basic soldering tools and skills, but those are great things to learn, and Rob will show you all the tricks.

Last, you'll need a way to cut the plywood and acrylic to fit inside the frame. If you have a woodworker friend, a tablesaw or bandsaw will do the job, or you can cut it yourself with a jigsaw—a small portable power tool that everyone needs. Finish off the look of your plywood panel with a couple coats of Danish oil.

That's really all there is to it. You can make your sign say whatever you want and change the lights to suit your mood.

# LASER CUTTERS WORK WONDERS

**1** **ELECTRONIC ART.** You don't have to be good at drawing to make amazing designs on the computer and turn them into precise drawing files for the laser cutter.   **2** **CUT OR ENGRAVE.** Depending on the power setting, a laser can engrave a design partway into any material or cut all the way through.

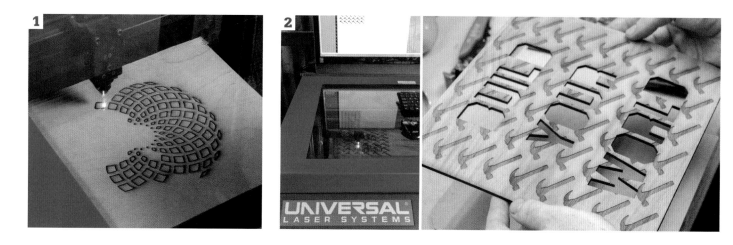

# GET READY TO CONNECT THE LIGHTS

The back of the Ribba frame makes the perfect base for attaching the LEDs and wires. Start by cutting the components to size and laying them out the way they'll be attached.

**1** **READY-MADE BOX.** Rob bought two IKEA Ribba frames, one black and one white. They are perfect for a small LED sign.   **2** **PLAN YOUR ARRAY.** Draw an outline of the letters or design on the frame's backboard, to show you where the LED strips should go.

**3** HERE'S WHAT THE FINISHED WIRING WILL LOOK LIKE. The LED controller will be connected to the LED strips by means of three separate triple wires. **4 CUT THE STRIPS TO SIZE.** The LED strips cut easily with scissors. Be sure to cut down the middle of the little copper pads, leaving half on each end of the strip. Also note the data direction indicated on each strip. **5 PREP THE WIRES.** Cut the triple wires to size and strip their ends. You can strip them with a razor or utility knife, or you can do all three wires instantly with a self-adjusting wire stripper like this one ($13).

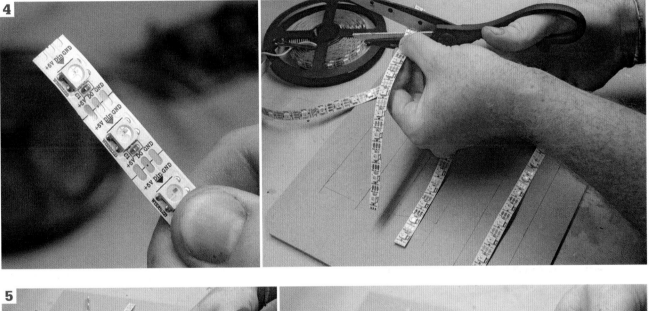

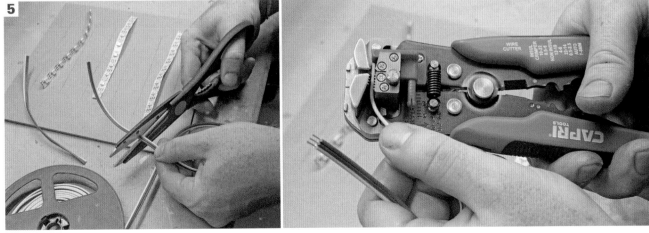

# SOLDER THE CONNECTIONS

The important thing here is that the red, green, and white wires run into all three strips in the same orientation, and that the strips face the right direction for proper data flow.

**1 FLUX GOES ON FIRST.** Melted solder will go wherever it finds this magic jelly, so dunk the ends of the wires into it and brush it on the little copper pads on the ends of the LED strips. **2 HEAT AND CLEAN THE IRON.** This soldering iron has a sponge built in. Wet it and use it to clean solder and flux off the tip of the hot iron. **3 FOUR-STEP PROCESS.** Melt some solder wire onto the tip of the gun (top left), drop a little onto each copper pad (top right), do the same on each wire (bottom left), then join the two and apply heat to fuse the solder together and attach the wires (bottom right). A little solder will do it; you don't want to connect one wire to the adjacent one.

# ATTACH THE LED CONTROLLER

Twist and solder the connections. Rob likes to cover them with heat-shrunk sleeves for a neat, tidy look, though electrical tape will work, too.

**1 JOIN THE LED WIRES.** Twist the three white wires together, then the greens and the reds, as shown. **2 SLIDE ON THE SLEEVES.** Cut a few short sections and slide them onto the wires of the LED controller. **3 ATTACH THE LED CONTROLLER.** Twist its wires onto the corresponding bunches of LED wires, as shown. **4 LOCK THEM TOGETHER.** Put flux on the connections and some solder on the iron. Touch the iron to the wires and the solder will flow out perfectly. **5 SHRINK-WRAP THE CONNECTIONS.** Pull on the protective sleeves and use a hair dryer or heat gun to shrink them tight.

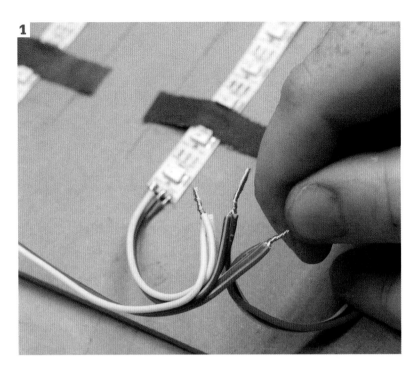

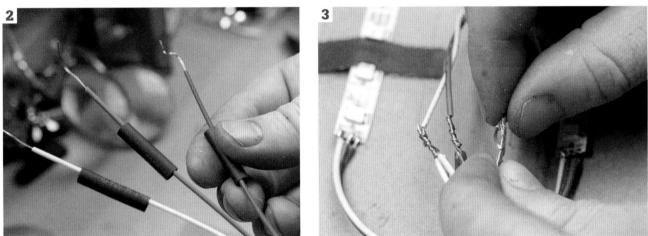

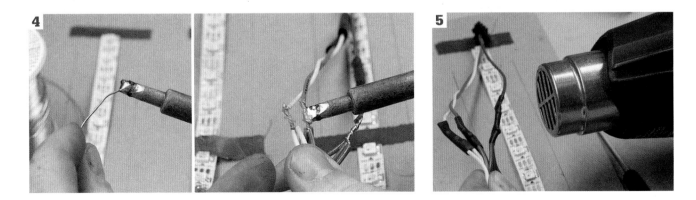

# FINISH OFF THE LIGHT PANEL

With all the connections made, you can attach everything to the backboard.

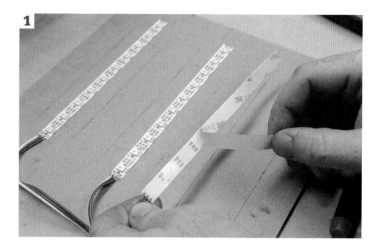

**1 LED STRIPS ARE SELF-ADHESIVE.** Just peel off the paper and press them into place. **2 STAPLE DOWN THE WIRES.** Use ⅜-in. staples to lock down all the wires so they don't obscure the lights. Then bend over the staple tips on the back and cover them with tape strips. **3 MAKE ROOM FOR THE POWER CORD.** The power cord needs to escape from a lower corner, so Rob lopped off a corner of the backboard.

# PUT IT ALL TOGETHER

With the help of the ready-made frame, assembly takes only a minute.

**1 HELP THE LASER.** There might be spots where the laser didn't cut all the way though. Flip over the panel and use an X-Acto knife to finish the job.

# Rob Leifheit

**B**ored with his job as a consultant at Wells Fargo, Rob Leifheit discovered LEDs and laser cutting on Reddit (reddit.com) and learned how to solder on YouTube. Soon he had cleared out a workshop space in the laundry room of his Los Angeles apartment, forcing himself to spend at least an hour there every day. "I stopped watching TV and getting high after work," he says.

When he was laid off by Wells Fargo, Rob spent his severance money on tools. He bought a laser cutter, a small CNC router, a 3-D printer, a tablesaw, clamps, and more—everything he needed to take his LED creations to the next level.

Before long, he found a creative day job too, producing graphics for live events. That taught him Adobe Illustrator, which dovetailed perfectly with his digital tools.

To build up his "10,000 hours," Rob has watched thousands of videos, taken online courses, and made a lot of signs. He highly recommends Lynda.com, which offers courses on all sorts of creative skills. Lately he's been taking woodworking classes to learn to fabricate better frames and cabinets for his work.

**2 ASSEMBLE THE SIGN.**
The mask goes in first, then the diffuser panel, and then an internal spacer (far left) that comes with the frame. Insert the backboard last (left), and fold down the little retainer clips at the back of the frame.

# FINISH OFF THE MASK

**1** **ATTACH LOOSE ELEMENTS.** To attach pieces of your design that aren't attached to the overall mask, like the insides of letters, save the supporting pieces and use them to locate the parts you want to keep. Rob attaches a little tape flag to the supporting piece, like this letter B, to make it easy to pull out later. **2** **SLICK TRICK.** Put Super Glue on the back of the piece you want to attach, drop it into place in the supporting piece, press it lightly against the acrylic panel below, wait a minute for the glue to grab, and then pull away the supporting piece as shown.

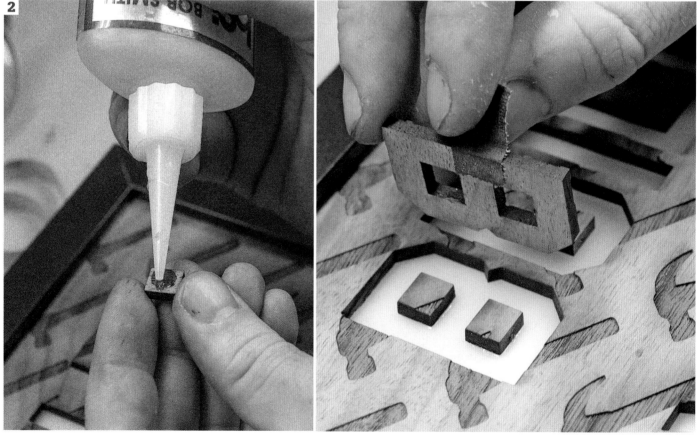

# 21

# use a vinyl cutter to brand your business (or hobby)

**with Chamisa Kellogg** ● While lasers and 3-D printers get all the press, the vinyl cutter stays mostly under the radar. It's a shame because this digitally driven cutter is less expensive, simpler to operate, and much more reliable than an entry-level 3-D printer that costs two or three times as much.

You can buy a very good vinyl cutter for under $300 and use it to make precise and intricate cuts in vinyl and paper stock of all kinds, opening the door to all sorts of projects.

**BUILD YOUR BRAND.** Chamisa used the same design to make a vinyl sign for her business and a vinyl mask for screen-printing on fabric. Vinyl signs like this one adhere seamlessly to most surfaces.

Chamisa uses the vinyl cutter to make stickers, stencils, and greeting cards as well as text and graphics for doors, walls, and windows. "The paper and vinyl parts can be applied to anything from scrapbooking projects to fine art to small business needs," she says. Self-adhesive, paper-backed vinyl is especially versatile and popular, and it's what Chamisa used for both projects shown here.

A vinyl stencil is yet another cool project you might try. To make a perfectly painted sign, for example, you just apply a vinyl stencil to wood and spray it with paint. The adhesive lets you remove and reattach stencils multiple times, so you can repeat the same image in multiple spots without paint leaking under the edges.

Like 3-D printers, CNCs, laser cutters, and other digital fabrication tools, vinyl cutters work off a digital drawing file, meaning you don't have to be an artist to use them. If you can copy or design something nice on the screen, the digital tool will cut it perfectly.

Chamisa recommends starting with a portable model like the Silhouette Cameo 3 ($270 on Amazon [amazon.com] at the time of writing). Electronic cutters work with a roll of paper or vinyl, so they can create designs of almost any length, but portable models usually top out at a 12-in.-wide roll. When you are ready to scale your designs beyond that limit, you can find large-scale cutters at makerspaces, colleges, and other community workshops. That's what Chamisa did for these projects.

## ONE DESIGN, MANY PRODUCTS

If you dive deeply into any of the media or modes in this book, there's a fair chance you might want to sell your work someday, so Chamisa and I thought it would be really cool to use a vinyl cutter to brand her business, and yours too.

She is a talented freelance illustrator and recently moved her office from her apartment to a rented space nearby. So it was the perfect time to dial in her branding, with signage and a way to make merchandise with the same logo. With the logo designed and refined, she then exported it into a variety of digital formats, letting her apply it easily to her website, cards, invoices, and everything else associated with her brand.

Even if you don't have an artisanal business in your future, the following projects will teach you super-useful skills. You'll learn how to make self-adhesive signs and transfer them seamlessly to walls and windows for a flawless professional look. You'll also learn how to cut a vinyl mask for screen-printing, so you can transfer that same picture of Gandalf or Yoda onto T-shirts, tote bags, posters, and more. It's just a taste of what you can do with a vinyl cutter.

If you aren't up to designing your own brand, you might have a friend who can help. Better yet, you can hire a freelance artist like Chamisa to help you convey the essence of your work in a compelling logo.

## BUYER'S GUIDE TO VINYL

Chamisa recommends visiting a sign-making shop for your supplies. Her local shop supplied all the items you see in use here, including transfer tape, a squeegee, inks, and various types of vinyl. Your brick-and-mortar buddies will find out what you want to use the vinyl for, tell you how long various products will last outdoors and in, and help you choose the right adhesive for the job. "Look for a place where you can buy vinyl by the yard, not a whole roll," she says. "It's nice to have different pieces to test and different colors to try."

You'll find all the supplies online too, but sign-making shops can usually come close to those prices, match supplies more closely to your needs, and give you lots of helpful info in the process.

For the projects here, Chamisa bought vinyl in 6-ft.-long pieces that are 24 in. wide to fit the vinyl cutter. But she selected two different finishes: interior matte black (Oracal product no. 631) for the wall sign

**SIMPLE SUPPLIES.** All you need for both vinyl projects are vinyl, transfer tape, a small dental tool, a screen for printing fabric, and two squeegees—one for transferring the vinyl sign to the wall and the other for screen-printing. You'll find everything at your local sign-making shop. You'll also need a vinyl cutter, of course.

and glossy vinyl for the screen-printing mask (Oracal product no. 651). These large, rolled-up pieces were only $7 each.

## THE BEAUTY OF THE TRANSFER

The way the self-adhesive vinyl parts and pieces are transferred to a surface is one of the coolest things I learned on this book journey. You'll pick up the particulars in the photos that follow, but here's how the magic works in brief. It's all about different levels of stickiness and a cool tool called transfer tape.

For starters, the vinyl cutter cuts through only the vinyl, not its paper backer. Once it's cut, you weed away all the parts you don't want, leaving the paper backer intact, and apply transfer tape to the front. The

transfer tape is the mystery ingredient that makes the magic happen. You use a plastic squeegee to apply it seamlessly to the front of the vinyl.

The key is how the transfer tape holds on to all the vinyl pieces a little more firmly than they stick to their slick paper backing. That makes the transfer simple and painless. You simply tape the top of the sign to the wall—vinyl, transfer tape, and all—and start peeling away the backer. At the exact same time, you rub the squeegee on the front of the transfer tape, applying it and all the vinyl pieces to the wall in the same process.

The self-adhesive vinyl sticks to a wall or window more powerfully than the pieces stuck to the paper backing, and it's even stronger than the transfer tape. Peel away the tape and the pieces are left in perfect position, dead-flat and bubble-free. It's amazing, and it's just one of the skills you'll pick up here.

# REFINE YOUR DESIGN

**1**

To turn an illustration into a logo and then a cutting path for the vinyl cutter, Chamisa used Adobe Illustrator. But there is free software that will do a similar job.

**1 IMPORT THE ART.** Chamisa started with a hand-drawn picture and used Illustrator's "image trace" function to turn it into a vector file, which is a series of shapes that can be scaled. Unlike an image, the smooth shapes will not get pixelated and choppy. **2 FIX THE SHAPES.** After it's converted, the image will have trapped white space and some disconnected lines. Those need to be filled in and connected, so you can create a continuous outline for the vinyl cutter. **3 REVERSE IT.** After filling in the center of the outline, Chamisa reversed the flower area to turn it white and delete it from the solid shape. In technical terms, the stroke of the shape should have no color, and the fill should be black. **4 ADD LETTERS.** These can be typed and styled in the same program. Once you're happy with the look, the letters need to be turned into shapes like everything else. The last step is exporting the document as a PDF and putting it on a flash drive.

**2**

**3**

**4**

# PUT IT ON VINYL

Chamisa took the flash drive to ADX, her local makerspace, and loaded the PDF into the software that guides the big vinyl cutter.

**1** **THE CUTTER DOES ALL THE WORK.** The computer runs a cutting program called Sure Cuts A Lot, which is easy to use. Loading the vinyl into the cutter is also easy. **2** **ONE DESIGN, TWO WAYS.** Chamisa printed the design small and *backward* on glossy vinyl to create the printing screen (left) and then much larger on matte vinyl for the wall sign (right). The vinyl cutter cuts only through the vinyl, not the backer paper.

# PEEL OFF THE PARTS YOU DON'T WANT

This process is called weeding. Dental tools, also available at your sign-making store, are a big help.

**1 WALL SIGN HAS LOTS TO REMOVE.** Hold down parts you want to keep as you peel away the big areas, and cut away large pieces as you go, to make the rest easier to handle. Leave the entire paper backing in place. **2 THE SCREEN IS EASIER.** Only the inner pieces need to come out of this pattern, to let the screen-printing ink pass through. Note that the printing screen is again backward.

# A SEAMLESS TRANSFER

This is the foolproof process pros use to transfer vinyl to walls, windows, and metal. Chamisa demonstrates it here on the screen-printing mask.

**1 ATTACH TRANSFER TAPE.** This comes in big rolls. Apply it to the front of the vinyl, starting from the top, using a squeegee (from the same sign-making shop). Avoid bubbles. **2 TRANSFER THE VINYL TO THE SCREEN.** Tape the top of the vinyl to the back of the screen and start peeling away the backer below, exposing the vinyl's adhesive to the screen. As you did with the transfer tape, use the squeegee to transfer the vinyl to the screen, working from the top down. Work gradually, preventing bubbles and wrinkles as you go. **3 PEEL AWAY THE TAPE AND VOILÀ.** The transfer tape comes away, leaving the vinyl attached perfectly.

# SCREEN-PRINTING A TOTE BAG

The same process will work for T-shirts and posters too. Be sure to choose the right ink and screen mesh for the type of material you are printing on. Chamisa used Pitch Black water-based ink from Green Galaxy.

**1 TEST RUN.** Test the process on paper first. Note the nice hinge mechanism that controls the screen in the makerspace's print shop, making it easy to align it on whatever you are printing. It also helps to have some sort of sticky surface on the table so your workpiece doesn't want to move. You can also tape it down.   **2 NOW THE REAL THING.** Chamisa aligned the bag with strips of tape before laying down another generous bead of ink and making a firm pass back and forth with the squeegee.
**3 PRINTED.** The ink still needs to dry and be heat-set with an iron, but the design looks great on the tote bag we bought at a local art-supply store.

# ATTACHING A WALL SIGN ━━━━━━━━━━

With lots of small pieces to transfer, the transfer tape is extra-critical here. But the process is the same as it was for the printing screen.

**1 GET READY.** Apply transfer tape to the front of the vinyl as before, and put a strip of painter's tape at the top edge to position the sign on the wall.   **2 TRANSFER.** Raise the sign and start peeling away the paper from the back side. Right away, start using the squeegee to apply the transfer tape (and the vinyl pieces along with it) to the wall, working your way slowly downward. **3 BIG REVEAL.** The vinyl pieces are now firmly and seamlessly stuck to the wall, so you can peel away the transfer tape, leaving behind a perfect sign. Now you know how the pros do it.

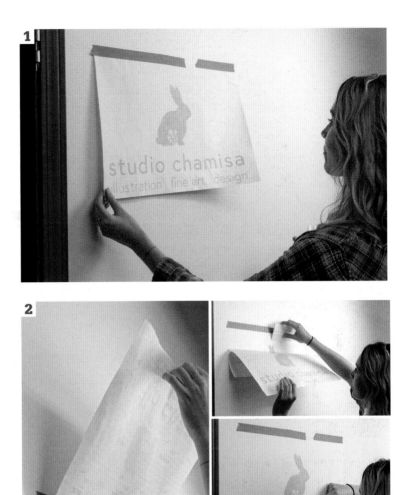

**FULL-TIME ARTIST.**
Chamisa Kellogg's
work appears in
books and magazines
and is sold as
individual pieces.
You can see more
of it at her website
(chamisakellogg.
com), including the
new branding she
developed for her
growing business.

I stand guard as my sister climbs the walnut tree to reach the highest berries. But the birds swoop and loop - they want the berries too.

# Chamisa Kellogg

Chamisa grew up in Sonoma County, Calif., where she attended a Waldorf school for grades K–12. She credits her career and her passion for creativity to the school's unique approach, which uses handwork to stimulate learning. Chamisa wrote and illustrated her own textbooks and maps and attended a regular handwork class that was a mix of sewing, knitting, woodworking, blacksmithing, even shoemaking and hat making, all tailored to the ages and capabilities of the students.

She discovered her love for drawing and watercolors in those early grades too, which led her to the famed Rhode Island School of Design, where she majored in illustration. After a stint as an art teacher at a private school in the Bay Area, Chamisa turned her side business as a freelance illustrator into a full-time job. It wasn't easy to make ends meet in one of the priciest places in North America. "It's hard to live in the Bay Area as an artist of any kind, both financially and in terms of how people value art," she says. "The only well-paid designers were UX [user experience] for digital."

Searching for a lower cost of living and a more welcoming culture, Chamisa headed north to Portland, Ore., in 2015, "looking for my people," she says. She found them at the local makerspace, where she now teaches classes. "There are tons of really knowledgeable people here who have helped me with my business and my craft."

**ADVICE FOR WOULD-BE MAKERS**

"Don't always try to make it perfect. Leave time for the experimentation part. If you want to come up with something that's really good, you need the Ugly Duckling phase, when you're thinking and rethinking something. It takes more than a couple hours."

# 9

# welding opens up a new world

**WITH ITS MYSTERIOUS** process, intense light, and shower of sparks, welding seems harder than it is and scarier too, warding many away from a wonderful new world of construction. To be fair, the equipment is a bit pricier than some of the other tools used in this book and the learning curve is longer, so I saved welding for the end of the book, as a jumping-off point to brave new worlds.

I think the closest comparison, in terms of skills and learning curve, is with woodworking. But steel has some major advantages. Compared to wood, it is available in a much wider range of ready-made forms—tubes, square and round; plates and bars, thick and thin; plus various beams and angle shapes. That means you don't necessarily have to shape steel to use it. You just cut it to length. To join the parts, however, unless you stick to nuts and bolts, you'll want to learn to weld.

In comparison to wood joinery, welded joints happen in seconds, meaning you can build surprisingly quickly. Better yet, steel needs very little finishing to look awesome. If you want color, there are methods for that, too.

This chapter is adapted from an article I wrote for *Woodcraft* magazine, introducing welding to woodworkers who might want to mix steel into their skill set. I haven't welded since tech school, where my machinist program offered a brief introduction. But I've been making wood furniture for 20 years, adding metal when I can, and always dreaming about adding

GREAT TEACHER. Longtime welder and instructor Kari Merkl breaks down the basics for beginners.

a welder to my arsenal. So I jumped at the chance to find an expert teacher and present the basics to a broad audience.

Lucky for me, my newly adopted hometown is a mecca for makers of all stripes. Kari Merkl (merkled.com) has been a professional welder for 18 years and teaching the craft for 6, so she is uniquely suited to break it down for beginners like us. I learned much of what is presented here during photo shoots at Kari's studio in Portland, Ore.

To present the basic techniques in a useful way, Kari and I built a piece of wood-and-steel furniture together. She welded the frame for a simple coffee table, and I added a top made of Port Orford cedar, a hard cedar native to Oregon. The clean, modern design is called a Parson's table, and you can make one in almost any size, for seating, dining, or whatever, with any sort of top. I used fresh wood on top, but reclaimed lumber would be a nice counterpart to the sleek steel.

To give a taste of what is possible when you master the basics, I reached out to Kari's colleagues and connections to create the gallery of pieces shown on p. 187.

Be warned: Once you have acquired the wizardly power of the welding gun, you probably won't stop at furniture. Sculpture, decorative items, funky fixtures for your tiny house—welded steel can do it all.

## SAFETY FIRST

The biggest challenge for would-be welders is the shop environment. Welding throws sparks, so you need to beware of everything within 10 ft. or 15 ft. If you can do your welding in a driveway or detached garage, all the better. Indoors, you need to shield any flammable areas or items with plastic welding curtains. These are affordable and come with grommet holes, so you can string them on wire and push them out of the way when they're not needed.

It also helps to have a metal table. That makes it easy to ground your work (as shown later). A clean wooden workbench is also spark-proof, but you'll need a layer of metal on top to prevent scorching. By the way, if you are a woodworker, with a dusty workspace, you'll need serious distance between your welding and woodworking zones, with welding curtains as spark shields. And this is probably a good time to get serious about dust collection.

The intense light and sparks are hostile to your person as well, so you'll need some basic gear to protect your body and eyes. It starts with a welding helmet. Kari recommends an auto-darkening lens, or shade 10 for a passive lens. To protect your body, leather and thick 100% cotton work best. The simplest

## LEARN AS YOU BUILD

To teach the basics, Kari built the base of a Parson's table, which has a simple rectilinear frame and a top that matches the length and width of the base; it makes a great first welding project. We sized our piece 20 in. wide by 48 in. long by 20 in. high for use as a coffee table, but you can make your table any size you want.

**WOOD MEETS METAL.** Any type of wood will work well with this steel base. I used Port Orford cedar, but reclaimed wood would look just as great.

approach is a leather apron and leather shoes, leather gloves designed for MIG (metal inert gas) welding, and thick cotton sleeves that pull over your arms. Shorts are a no-no.

Also, while you can get by breathing welding fumes for a few minutes, the gases are ultimately toxic, so a respirator is also recommended. Here's the rest of a basic safety checklist:

- Have a fire extinguisher on hand.
- Clear all flammable materials, including open trash cans.
- Make sure there is good ventilation.
- Don't weld outside in the rain.
- Don't use an extension cord on your welder.
- Avoid welding plated, galvanized, or painted steel.

## CUTTING STEEL AND BASIC METALWORK

After safety, the first step is cutting steel to size. The least expensive option for clean cuts is a metal cutoff saw, a version of a miter saw that uses an abrasive wheel and is designed to resist hot, flying sparks. These saws also have a built-in vise for holding steel firmly. You can find new models for under $100, but expect to pay a bit more for quality and durability. Abrasive cutoff saws leave a good-size burr on cut edges, which you'll have to sand or file off afterward.

The best option for clean, square cuts on steel is a horizontal bandsaw. A basic model is around $300 from Grizzly (grizzly.com). These are gravity driven, meaning you just clamp one or more lengths of stock in place, hit the switch, lower the blade down to the metal, and walk away. Industrial models include a coolant system, but you probably won't need that for the hollow tubes and thin stock used for furniture making.

As for the other tools, you probably have a few of them already: files, pliers, squares, tape measure, and so on. That said, there are some specialty clamps and other welding accessories you'll pick up along the way.

## WELDERS AND WELDING: WHY WIRE-FEED?

Now to the welder itself. There are different ways to weld, from bare bones to new school, and each approach has its pluses and minuses. Oxy-acetylene welding uses explosive gas, stored in a big tank; stick welding won't work on thin metal furniture parts; and tungsten inert gas (TIG) welding creates wonderful joints with almost no sparks but is tricky to learn.

For basic welding of mild steel, especially for non-pros, you can't beat MIG, an easy-to-learn form of wire-feed arc welding in which the current between a consumable wire electrode and a metal workpiece causes the wire and surrounding metal parts to melt and join together. A mix of argon and carbon dioxide ($CO_2$) comes from a tank, passing through the gun as you weld and shielding the process from contaminants in the air that hinder it.

To keep things as simple as possible, new welders should stick to mild steel, with a "cold-rolled" finish. In fact, this might be the only metal you end up using. Cold-rolled steel has a sleek surface, is widely available in dimensionally accurate shapes, and most important, is easy to weld with a basic, affordable machine like the one Kari uses here.

For our table, Kari demonstrated an even simpler version of wire-feed welding that uses wire with a flux core, with the heated flux making a tiny plume that does the shielding (instead of an inert gas like argon). The downside of this method is slightly rougher welds plus more spatter and fumes, but it lets you get started without the big tank. Another plus to flux-cored wire welding is that it works better outdoors, where even a slight breeze can dissipate argon gas and disrupt its shielding function.

The really good news is that a solid entry-level MIG welder costs under $500 and will do both MIG (with gas) and flux-cored (without it). And it will work on common 115-volt power. Kari has had great experience with Hobart welders and, at a slightly lower price point, Craftsman models, too. She warns against super-cheap welders from bargain outlets.

Most welders come with the gun that feeds the wire (and gas in MIG mode) and a ground clamp that attaches either to the metal table or the parts themselves, to complete the circuit and make welding happen when you pull the trigger on the gun. It's helpful to buy a few extra tips for the gun, as these degrade over time and start adhering to the weld.

## PREPPING THE PARTS

The initial steps are the same for any welding method. The first is cutting the parts to size, using one of the tools mentioned earlier, and deburring the cut surfaces. A benchtop belt or disk sander works great, while a mill bastard file is slow but effective. Kari formed a tiny bevel around all of the cut edges of her parts, and the weld easily filled those bevels while creating a raised bead.

A next-level technique would be to grind deeper bevels at all the joints, fill them with the weld, and then grind the beads flush afterward. But grinding requires a whole new set of skills and tools, and there is nothing wrong with leaving the welds visible and embracing the aesthetic. The upside to this approach is that cleanup requires only hand tools (as shown later).

The welding process is hampered by contaminants, so the next step is cleaning dirt and grease off all of the steel parts. Solvents like lacquer thinner and denatured alcohol work well, but Kari prefers Simple Green, which does a similar job without the fumes.

If you'll be drilling holes in the parts, as Kari did in the upper frame for attaching the wood top, now is the time, while the parts are easy to handle. If you have a drill press and a set of standard twist bits, you are all set, though a handheld drill will work, too.

Start each hole by dimpling the metal with a center punch, and then clamp the part firmly in place

and drip some oil into the hole as you drill. Do not try to hold the parts by hand, as the bit can grab the piece hard as it breaks through the bottom of the hole, causing the whole thing to climb up the bit and spin out of your grasp.

## HOLDING PARTS IN PLACE

The way most welding works is that the parts are clamped in precisely the position you want them, and then you make a few small tack welds to hold them in place. Then the clamps can come off so you can make full welds at every joint. Much like building wood furniture, you weld subassemblies first and then join them to make the whole thing. For our table base, we welded two legs and an end rail to create one end, then the other two legs and end rail, and finally, we connected those two subassemblies with the two long rails to complete the base.

Woodworking bar clamps with metal jaws can work to hold parts in place, but Kari used a couple of other tools and methods for the job (see p. 196), including steel bars clamped across corners to keep parts square.

## helpful tips for happy welds

A good weld is a dance of voltage, motion, welding wire, and molten steel, and getting it right requires practice—to build muscle and eye memory, gain experience, and learn some basic troubleshooting. On the other hand, practice costs next to nothing—just wire, scrap steel, and electricity.

Here are Kari's best tips for getting through your learning curve and having success as early as possible.

- Start by reading the manual for your welder to get the right settings for the thickness of material you are welding. Now ground the work. You can attach the grounding clamp to the parts you are working on, but usually it's easier to simply ground the

# MORE WELDED INSPIRATION

There are an endless number of things you can build from steel. Here are just a few examples, from Kari Merkl and others. All photos are courtesy of the makers.

Kari Merkl made this pot rack, stool, and bench, which has a steel base and cherry slats.

This outdoor table is by David Bertman of Portland, Ore. (davidbertmandesigns.com).

Jacob Wener, of Modern Industry (modernindustrydesign.com) in Chicago, built this low stool.

These side tables and coat rack are by Matthew Philip Williams (matthewmatthewmatthew.com) of Portland. The steel parts on the coat rack are powder-coated, which is a very durable color finish.

metal table the parts are sitting on. Trim the wire so it sticks out about ¼ in. from the nozzle cap on the gun, and get ready to weld.

- For best control, put both hands on the gun—for righties, the right hand on the trigger and the left hand as a guide—and move from left to right, "dragging" the weld along behind the gun. Once you get comfortable, you'll be able to both push and drag a weld, but going from left to right (or vice versa for lefties) is a great way to learn, and more important, to start learning how to see

> **Pretty soon, you'll recognize the sound a happy welder makes: It's like the sizzle of frying bacon (always a nice thought).**

what's happening.

- The most critical part of the learning curve is training your brain to look through the dark lens and intense light to see the weld area—seeing a bigger circle, basically, not just the short, bright arc of electricity. It takes time, but eventually you'll be able to see what's happening at the tip of the wire and adjust your technique for better results. Don't be afraid of the bright light; the right lens will protect your eyes.

- For best results, hold the welding gun at a 45° angle to the work, but aligned with the direction you are moving. The idea is to hold the gun so you can see the tip of the welding wire, but not so steep that the wire misses the weld puddle. Another key is to maintain a consistent distance between the tip of the gun and the workpiece—about ⅛ in. Feel free to rest the side of the nozzle cap on the piece to maintain that distance.

- Now, with your welding hood down, pull the trigger and make a straight line to begin. This will help you get a feeling for the speed. You should be able to see the arc through your lens when the welder is on. Resist the urge to release the trigger when the sparks fly, and remember that the trigger is on/off, not an adjustable accelerator.

- Once you can consistently produce a straight, solid line, try adding the swirling motion that creates a strong, full welding bead (see photos on p. 194). Choose either the half-moon or drag-and-loop patterns and try to make a consistent bead between ¼ in. and ½ in. wide.

- Work on staying one step ahead of the molten puddle as you move back and forth to create the weld. Don't outrace the puddle and don't go too slowly. Find the flow; it's like dancing.

- Practice, practice, practice until you can really see what you are doing. This will be a sign you are getting the hang of it and have control.

- Last, practice vertical and horizontal welds on various joints. This table is an example: It uses butt joints and tee joints and requires horizontal and vertical movement along the various seams. And don't forget to practice "tack" welds: short, 1-second to 2-second welds that hold material together but can be broken if needed.

## signs of trouble and success

Too many sparks are a general sign of trouble: You could be holding the tip of the gun too far from the work or have the feed rate set too slow or too fast. Another sign you are holding the gun too far from the work is a long wire left at the tip when you finish the weld.

Pretty soon, you'll recognize the sound a happy welder makes: It's like the sizzle of frying bacon (always a nice thought). Finally, as with any new endeavor, accept imperfection as part of your journey.

## WELD IN STAGES TO MANAGE HEAT AND STRESS

Welding and heat apply tension to a joint and can pull it out of square, but there is a smart process for preventing that. By tacking one corresponding part of each joint at a time—say the top-facing seam—moving in an orderly direction around the assembly, you are applying only small forces at first and balancing those forces as you go. You are also letting the heat disperse before you return to the same area.

With everything tacked and stable, you follow the same path around the assembly as you make full welds, one seam of a joint at a time—such as the top-facing seams or inside corners—always moving in the same direction around the assembly to keep track of your progress. A nice rhythm develops and soon the whole frame is done.

## FINISHING TOUCHES

A simple cleanup goes a long way toward making the welds look clean and consistent. Especially with flux-cored wire, each weld will be caked with slag, with little beads of metal splatter nearby. But both of those issues are easy to deal with.

The splatter comes off with a stiff metal scraper, like the end of a piece of bar stock. The next steps are to scour away the slag and welding residue with a wire brush. Small abrasive hand pads, like the ones from 3M, work well to smooth away any scratches and finish the job.

The simple cleanup and buffing paves the way for an equally simple finish—just two coats of paste wax, which add a soft sheen and a measure of protection against rust and corrosion from finger oil.

Of course, there are as many wonderful ways to finish metal as there are wood, maybe more. For opaque color, an industrial-quality spray paint, such as Rust-Oleum, can be surprisingly durable, especially if you prime first. But many prefer powder coating, an electrical process that creates an incredibly tough, smooth color coat. You'll have to find a pro shop to do that for you.

Heat alone will darken steel. For the blue-black tones of gun-bluing and a wide variety of other patinas, Kari recommends products from Birchwood Casey (birchwoodcasey.com).

Finally, there all sorts of plugs and inserts available for finishing off the ends of standard steel tubing. McMaster-Carr (mcmaster.com) is a great source. For our table, I chose plastic inserts to fit the tubes and steel feet that thread into those inserts and then adjust to level the legs.

## ADDING WOOD TO METAL

Obviously, you need some way to fasten your wood parts to the metal ones. The easiest route is screwing through the metal into the wood and finding a way to hide the screw heads. For tables like ours it is simple. Kari just drilled through the frame rails so I could drive screws from below.

In other cases, it makes sense to weld small tabs inside the frame and screw through those. The ability to weld gives you all sorts of options for attachment points.

Of course, design matters, too. In this case, I wanted the top to be the same thickness as the frame, for a modern, unified look, but I also wanted it to float a little off the top rails, to let both parts stand out as separate. So I made the top $1/8$ in. extra thick and used the router to cut a $1/8$-in. notch, called a rabbet, in the lower edge of the top before attaching it.

This project was a great collaboration, but I can't wait to get my own welder and start making sparks. My plan is to turn some old steel machine parts into sculpture. What's yours?

# GEARING UP

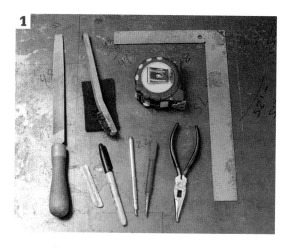

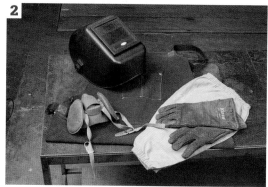

You'll need some basic hand tools for metalworking, a few key safety items, and a welder.

**1 A FEW HAND TOOLS.** Clockwise from left are a mill bastard file, a wire brush and abrasive pad, a tape measure and framing square, needle-nose pliers with a wire cutter, two types of center punches for drilling, and two markers for steel: a Sharpie and soapstone.
**2 PROTECTION AGAINST LIGHT, SPARKS, AND FUMES.** A basic kit includes a welding helmet, thick cotton sleeves, leather welding gloves, a leather apron, and a respirator. **3 BEST TOOL FOR CUTTING STEEL TO LENGTH.** The cheapest option is a metal cutoff saw with an abrasive wheel, and the best is a horizontal bandsaw like this one. **4 GREAT OVERALL SETUP.** A plastic welding curtain shields flammable areas from sparks and others in the room from UV light, while cotton and leather shield the welder. A steel table is spark-proof, of course, but also makes it easy to ground the work, an essential for arc welding.

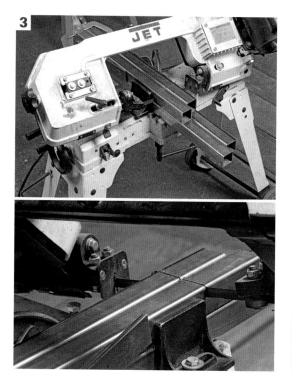

# GOOD WELDERS FOR LESS

If you stick to steel, you can do great work with a wire-feed welder. The most basic models use wire with a flux core to create the small but critical gas plume that shields the welding process, while MIG welders add a tank of argon gas for the same purpose, offering better control and smoother results.

**1 SOLID CHOICE.** You can get a gasless wire-feed welder for under $300, but a few bucks more will buy you a model that will also convert to MIG welding, for cleaner welds. Hobart welders like the Handler 130 work in both modes and have separate adjustments for wire feed rate and voltage/heat, giving you excellent control. The 130 can also weld stainless steel. **2 EVEN THE MOST BASIC WELDER CAN DO THE JOB.** On this table, Kari proved that even an old basic Craftsman wire welder—offering combined settings for feed and heat—can make serviceable welds with flux-cored wire. **3 WHAT A LITTLE MORE MONEY GETS YOU.** At left is a weld Kari made using flux-cored wire, and at right is a MIG weld, shielded by argon gas. In short, MIG makes it easier to produce a smooth weld and creates less spatter, though those little beads are easy to scrape off.

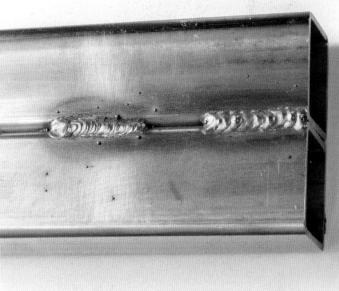

# 22

# classic table teaches the basic techniques

**with Kari Merkl** • While building the base of a Parson's-style coffee table, Kari teaches the basics of wire-feed welding, from cutting and drilling steel to mastering the welding process itself. Along the way, you'll learn basic safety, tools and supplies needed, how to approach a large assembly in a logical way, and how to complete a piece of welded furniture by adding a lovely wood top and nice feet. With Kari clearing away the mystery around this amazing craft, you'll be inspired to give it a try.

## PREPPING PARTS

Before you plug in the welder and flip down your helmet, you have some cleanup, cutting, and drilling to do.

**1 CLEAN STEEL BEFORE WELDING.** Simple Green or basic solvents will remove grease and grime for better welds. **2 MEASURE AND MARK.** After cutting one end square and clean, mark your parts for cutting to length. There are soapstone markers for steel, but a Sharpie shows up better. **3 CHOP PARTS TO LENGTH.** The horizontal bandsaw makes it easy to clamp together multiple parts, walk away, and let gravity do the job, but a more affordable metal cutoff saw also works well.

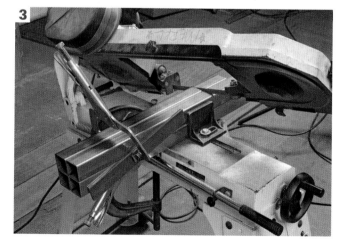

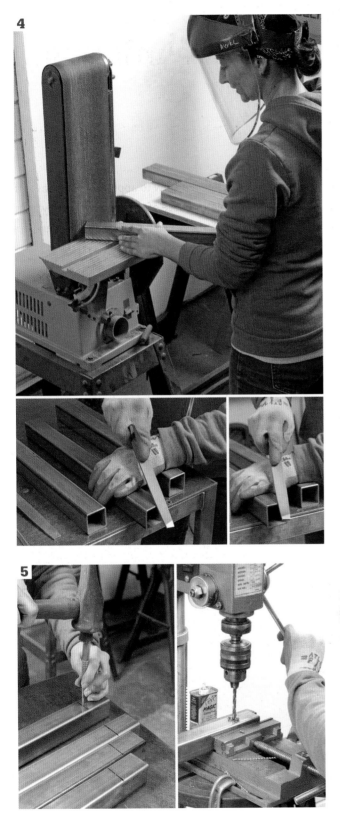

**4 DEBURR AND CHAMFER.** Any cutoff tool will leave razor-sharp edges and burrs. Sand or file those to create small chamfers. **5 DRILLING METAL.** On this table base, the top rails need holes for screwing on the wood top. Drill those while the parts are separate. Start with a center punch, making a small dimple at the layout marks, and use a vise or clamps to hold the stock safely while drilling. Use a twist drill at a slow speed, lubricating the bit with oil as you go. If you use a handheld drill, work up to a large hole with a series of smaller ones, to prevent the drill from grabbing hard when it breaks through the other side. **6 COUNTERSINK HOLES TO CLEAN THEM UP.** Remove the small burrs from drilling using a countersink bit. Go deeper if you want the screws to sit flush.

# PRACTICE MAKES PERFECT

Welding is a simple process: An arc of electricity creates high heat that melts the wire and the steel on both sides of a seam, creating a molten puddle that cools to join the parts. But it takes practice to master the movement and learn to see what's happening at the tip of the gun.

**1** KEY PARTS OF THE WELDER. To complete the circuit, you need a ground clamp, attached to the workpieces or the steel table below them, and a spool gun, broken down here into its key parts (from left): the nozzle and contact tip, which slip over the wire and screw onto the end of the gun. **2** BEST ANGLE. Snip off the wire about ¼ in. from the tip and hold the spool gun at a 45° angle to the work, more or less, with the nozzle resting on the surface to help you maintain that angle and the distance between the wire and the work. The angled gun also helps you see the tip as you work. **3** START WITH STRAIGHT LINES. Start by pulling the trigger and dragging the gun in a straight line to dial in your pace and the rate the wire is being fed (adjustable on the welder). Kari purposely moved the gun too fast on the first weld, too slowly on the second, and just about right on the last. **4** ADD THE SWIRL. Welders build up a strong bead by swirling the tip of the gun as they drag it along. Some do the half-moons Kari is drawing here (left), and others prefer the drag-and-loop pattern just below. Try both and pick your favorite. Practice on scrap steel until you get a full bead that looks something like the one shown at right.

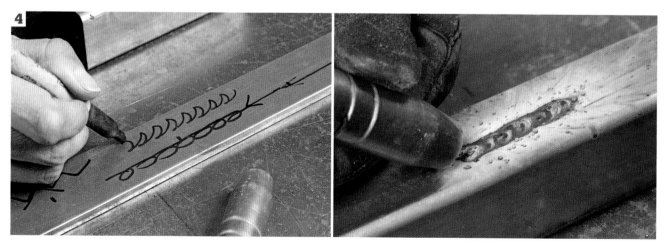

**5 SIGNS OF TROUBLE.** The top weld is thin and bumpy because the wire feed rate was too slow; the lack of a heat ring indicates that voltage/heat was too low. The oversize heat ring and melty look of the bottom weld are sure signs that the heat/voltage was too high.

**5**

# basic troubleshooting guide

Start with the settings the manufacturer recommends for a given material thickness. Then use this chart to adjust those settings and your technique. Be sure to clear splatter off the nozzle cap every so often.

| PROBLEM | CAUSE |
|---------|-------|
| Too many sparks | Wire setting is too fast or too slow or wire is too far from workpiece |
| Wire melting before hitting the weld | Wire setting is too slow |
| Weld buildup | Not enough heat (voltage) or wire feed too fast |
| Blistering or burn through | Voltage setting too hot |
| No heat ring | Voltage setting too low |
| Porous weld | Shielding gas not on or has run out (not a problem with flux-cored wire) |
| Not making spark when trigger is pulled | Grounding clamp not attached |
| Welding wire very long when done | Gun held too far from workpiece |

# WELDING A FRAME

To set up for success, you need to lock down the parts square to each other. Welding puts pressure on the joints, though, so there is an important sequence to follow to keep those parts aligned as you weld them.

**1 SQUARE AND CLAMP.** It's much easier to join subassemblies first. These little magnet clamps are quick and easy to use (top), grabbing the steel table and steel parts at the same time, but woodworking clamps with steel jaws also work well. So do steel corner clamps designed for miters. Make sure the parts are square to each other before you grab the gun. **2 TACK FIRST.** Move around the assembly, making small tack welds. The high heat of welding can distort a frame, moving it out of alignment, but the tack welds lock the parts in place without introducing excessive heat. The tack welds will be cool by the time you return with full welds. **3 NOW THE FULL WELDS.** Before unclamping the parts, come back and do full welds. After that, you can reposition the parts and do the inside corners and backside seams, again tacking first at each location before circling back to do the full welds.

**4**

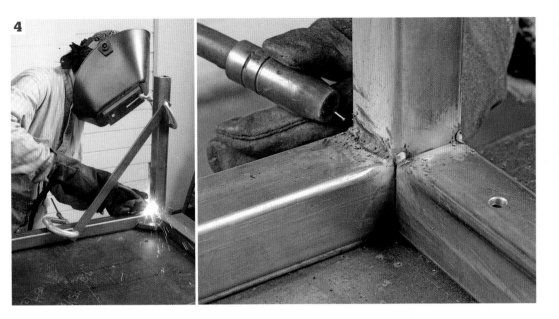

**4 ADD THE FINAL PARTS.** Kari used thin metal bars to hold the assemblies square for welding. Wood sticks would work, too. The same tack-and-weld process applies.

# Kari Merkl

Kari Merkl is the owner of Merkled Studio in Portland, Ore., where she designs and fabricates custom metal furniture, fixtures, and small batches of products for residential and commercial spaces—work she has done for 18 years. She began her career in architecture, but soon realized she wanted to know more about how things are made. So she talked her way into a design/manufacturing firm in Denver, she says, and started learning how to build with wood and metal. Later, she opened her own design-build shop. Her varied background lets her move between the worlds of conceptual design and hands-on fabrication. Over the past 6 years, Kari has also been teaching MIG and TIG welding and says she loves getting people excited about the possibilities of metal, especially other women.

# FINISHING TOUCHES FOR STEEL

Compared to wood, steel is easy to clean up and finish.

**1 SCRAPE THE SPLATTER.** Flux-core wire splatters a bit, but the little beads are easy to knock off with any steel edge.  **2 BRUSH THE SLAG.** Welding also leaves some slag and flux residue, but it comes off easily too, with a wire brush this time.  **3 BUFF AND FINISH.** Abrasive pads—rough then fine—remove the rest of the heat marks and the scratches from brushing, and one or two coats of paste wax are all the finish you need.

# ADD FEET AND A TOP

**1 CAPS AND FEET.** There are dozens of caps and feet available online for all sorts of steel tube sizes and shapes. We used the type that tap in firmly with a mallet and are threaded for levelers.    **2 THE TOP JUST SCREWS ON.** I used a router to make a little notch all around the bottom of the wood top, to create a gap between the steel and wood. After applying a polyurethane finish, I drilled pilot holes in the wood and drove screws through the frame to attach it. I assembled this top by gluing two new boards together, but reclaimed wood would also be beautiful, as would any wide slab of wood, trimmed to size with a circular saw.

# INDEX